OXFORD
Quick

take off in

Latin American Spanish

Rosa María Martín and Martyn Ellis

OXFORD
UNIVERSITY PRESS

OXFORD
UNIVERSITY PRESS

Great Clarendon Street, Oxford OX2 6DP

Oxford University Press is a department of the University of Oxford.
It furthers the University's objective of excellence in research, scholarship,
and education by publishing worldwide in

Oxford New York

Auckland Bangkok Buenos Aires Cape Town Chennai
Dar es Salaam Delhi Hong Kong Istanbul Karachi Kolkata
Kuala Lumpur Madrid Melbourne Mexico City Mumbai Nairobi
São Paulo Shanghai Singapore Taipei Tokyo Toronto

Oxford is a registered trade mark of Oxford University Press
in the UK and in certain other countries

Published in the United States
by Oxford University Press Inc., New York

British Library Cataloguing in Publication Data
Data available

Library of Congress Cataloging in Publication Data
Data available

ISBN 0-19-860657-5 (Book and CDs)
ISBN 0-19-860656-7 (Book and cassettes)
ISBN 0-19-860739-3 (Book only)

3 5 7 9 10 8 6 4 2

Latin American Spanish consultants: Lydia Goldsmith, Gerardo Vásquez Gómez
Teaching consultant: Jenny Ollerenshaw
Copy-editing and proofreading: Susan Wilkin, Elspeth Anderson, Jane McCauley
Audio Production: Daniel Pageon, Actors World Production Ltd
Design: Paul Saunders Typesetting: Pantek Arts Ltd
Series Editor: Natalie Pomier
Printed in Spain by Book Print S.L.

Contents

Welcome to Quick Take Off In Latin American Spanish!

Whatever your reason for traveling to Central or South America, whether for a break, a vacation, or a business trip, you'll need some basic Spanish to get by. Using this course, you'll learn enough Spanish to travel around and make the most of your stay. Learning to communicate in another language may seem challenging at first, but it's also a rewarding and enriching experience, as well as being the best passport to discovering another culture.

A little language goes a long way

Even if you feel unsure about your ability to form correct, complete Spanish sentences, you'll find you can communicate with just a few words. Don't worry about getting things wrong at this stage – people will still be able to understand you. They'll also appreciate the fact that you're making the effort to speak Spanish. The important thing is to build up your confidence so that you're not afraid of getting into conversations with native speakers. After you've taken that first step, you'll feel your confidence grow by the minute.

When listening to the recorded material, don't expect to understand everything first time round. Play the same dialogue several times, and you'll find something new in it each time. Learn to make maximum use of all the clues you can pick up. Listen closely to the speakers' voices. Do they sound happy, irritated, calm, etc? We have left pauses on the recording for you to repeat phrases or take part in conversations using prompts in English. These pauses are fairly short but bear in mind that you can always pause the recording if you need more time to speak.

Using this course

You can use this course in two different ways. You can start with unit 1 and work through the six thematic units of the course. This will teach you the basics of the language through dialogues, activities, and information on Spanish usage. If you're in a real hurry or just want to brush up your existing knowledge of Spanish, you can start with essential phrases in the survival guide and then dip in and out of the course by selecting the thematic units which are most relevant to your situation.

You will find the survival guide at the end of the second cassette or CD. You can listen to the phrases and repeat them while reading them on the credit-card size survival guide supplied in your pack. You can also use it for revision or to test yourself after you've completed the six units. The survival guide phrases can also be found in the Quick Reference section of your book, with some extra phrases.

When traveling, just slip the survival guide into your wallet or purse and you'll have all the essential phrases at your fingertips: from 'hello' to 'can you help me?', together with a list of numbers and handy conversion charts.

At the end of the book, you'll find a Spanish-English vocabulary list, a glossary of basic grammatical terms cross-referred to by means of asterisks in the body of the course, and a very short grammar summary. You'll also find an answer key section, containing answers to all the activities, except those found on the recording.

Pronunciation

Generally speaking, Spanish pronunciation is straightforward. The important thing to remember is that all letters are pronounced except **h** when it occurs at the beginning of a word, and that vowels are always short. Other sounds that sometimes cause difficulty are the **j**, **ge**, and **gi** sounds, the **r** and **rr** sounds, the **ci** and **ce** sounds, the **ñ** sound, and the **ll** sound.

Vowels

In Spanish, each vowel is pronounced consistently, and they are always short. Vowels can also be combined, for example **ei**, **ie**, **iu**, **ue**, to create a specific sound (see below). The secret of good Spanish pronunciation is to say the vowels as short as possible.

vowel	example	approximate English sound
a	c**a**sa, p**a**dre	c**a**t
e	l**e**che, tr**e**n	l**e**t
i	f**i**n, d**i**st**i**nto	k**i**t
o	c**o**che, h**o**nrad**o**	h**o**t
u	**u**no, fr**u**ta	g**oo**d

vowel combinations

e + i	ac**ei**te	w**ai**t
i + e	t**ie**ne	**ye**t
i + u	c**iu**dad	**you**
u + e	b**ue**no	w**e**t

Consonants

Most consonants are pronounced as in English. The exceptions are as follows:

c + i/e	is pronounced like the English **s** in **s**un: **c**ine, **c**entro.
g + i/e	is pronounced in the same way as **j**: **g**ente, **g**igante
h	is not pronounced: **h**ermano, **h**elado
j	has no English equivalent, but is similar to **ch** in lo**ch**: **j**amón, **j**ota
ñ	is pronounced like the **ni**o of on**i**on: ni**ñ**o, pi**ñ**a
r	at the beginning of a word and after **l**, **n**, **s** is rolled: **r**ojo, son**r**isa
r	between vowels is softer: pe**r**o, ca**r**o
rr	is rolled: pe**rr**o, ca**rr**o
v	is pronounced more like the English **b** in **b**ed: **v**acaciones, **v**iejo
z	is pronounced like the English **s** in **s**un: **z**apato

Combinations:

gu + a	is pronounced like the **gu** in **Gu**atemala: **gu**apo, **gu**ardia
gu + i/e	is pronounced like the English **g** in **g**ood: **gu**erra, **gu**itarra
ll	is pronounced like the English **lli** in mi**lli**on: **ll**ave, ca**ll**e
qu	is pronounced like the English **k**: **qu**eso, **qu**iero

Stress

Words in Spanish are stressed as follows:
- word ending in a vowel or **n** or **s** – on the penultimate syllable (last syllable from the end): **ca**sa, **quie**ren, **co**mes
- word ending in any other consonant – on the last syllable: habl**ar**, sal**ud**
- irregular stress is shown by an accent: **Mé**xico

Quick Reference Section

This section provides you with essential everyday Latin American Spanish phrases which you may need to say or understand in real-life situations. They are listed thematically, with their English equivalents and can be used independently of the book. The unit number after the phrases indicates the ones which are used in context in the course and where to find them. In addition, there are extra thematic areas not covered in the book, which you can find here. The phrases are also on the recording, so you can listen to the phrases and repeat them while reading them in your book. This will also help you to familiarize yourself with how everyday Latin American Spanish really sounds. If you don't have enough time to practice from the book first, work through this section before looking at the units in detail, and select those which are most relevant to your particular situation.

Whatever stage of the course you are studying, use this section as a quick reference and practice repeating the phrases to improve your pronunciation. You can also use it for reviewing and to test yourself.

Meeting, greetings, and saying goodbye

hola	hi there	➤ Unit 1
adiós	goodbye	➤ Unit 1
buenos días	good morning	➤ Unit 1
buenas tardes	good afternoon/good evening (early)	➤ Unit 1
buenas noches	good evening (late)/goodnight	➤ Unit 1
¿cómo está?	how are you? (*formal*)	➤ Unit 1
¿qué tal?	hi, how are you doing? (*informal*)	➤ Unit 1
hasta luego	see you later	➤ Unit 1
hasta pronto	see you soon	
hasta mañana	see you tomorrow	
bien	fine	➤ Unit 1
¿y usted?	and yourself? (*formal*)	➤ Unit 1
¿y tú?	and yourself? (*informal*)	➤ Unit 1

Being polite

gracias	thank you	➤ Unit 2
de nada	you're welcome	➤ Unit 3
por favor	please	➤ Unit 2

perdón	pardon me	
disculpe	excuse me; *also* I apologize	➤ Unit 3
lo siento	I'm sorry	➤ Unit 5
no, gracias	no, thank you	
sí, por favor	yes, please	
con mucho gusto	I'd love to; with pleasure	

Communicating

¿habla español?	do you speak Spanish? (*formal*)	
¿hablas español?	do you speak Spanish? (*informal*)	
un poco	a little bit	
no comprendo	I don't understand	
hable más despacio, por favor	speak slowly, please	
¿puede repetir?	could you repeat that?	
¿cómo se llama?	what's your name? (*formal*)	➤ Unit 1
¿cómo te llamas?	what's your name? (*informal*)	➤ Unit 1
me llamo …	my name is …	➤ Unit 1
mi nombre es …	my name is …	➤ Unit 5
encantado/a	delighted to meet you	
mucho gusto	pleased to meet you	➤ Unit 1
¿de dónde es (usted)?	where do you come from? (*formal*)	➤ Unit 1
¿de dónde eres (tú)?	where are you from? (*informal*)	➤ Unit 1
soy de Boston	I come from Boston	➤ Unit 1
soy estadounidense	I'm American	➤ Unit 1
soy de los Estados Unidos	I'm from the United States	➤ Unit 1
soy inglés	I'm English (*for a man*)	➤ Unit 1
soy inglesa	I'm English (*for a woman*)	➤ Unit 1

On the phone

¿puedo hablar con el señor …/la señora …?	I'd like to speak to Mr/Mrs …
¿puedo dejar un recado?	can I leave a message?
hablaré más tarde	I'll call back later
¿quiere dejar un recado?	would you like to leave a message?
hable al oír la señal	please speak after the tone
el número está fuera de servicio	number no longer in use
(usted) se ha equivocado de número	sorry, you've got the wrong number
el código del distrito	area code
el número de teléfono	telephone number
bueno	hello (*on the phone*)

In hotels

quiero reservar un cuarto individual/doble	I'd like to book a single/double room	➤ Unit 5
con baño	with bathroom	➤ Unit 5
¿A qué hora se sirve el desayuno?	when is breakfast served?	
¿Está incluido el desayuno (en el precio)?	is breakfast included (in the price)?	➤ Unit 5
la regadera no funciona	the shower doesn't work	➤ Unit 5
la lámpara está rota	the lamp is broken	➤ Unit 5
la tina está sucia	the bath is dirty	➤ Unit 5
faltan toallas	there aren't any towels	➤ Unit 5
hay mucho ruido	it's very noisy	➤ Unit 5
¿puedo pagar con Visa?	can I pay by Visa?	➤ Unit 5

Changing money

¿dónde puedo cambiar dinero?	where can I change money?
puede cambiar dinero en el banco/la casa de cambio	you can change money at the bank/currency exchange
¿a cómo está el cambio?	what's the exchange rate?
quiero cambiar cien dólares a pesos	I'd like to change $100 into pesos
¿hay comisión?	do you charge commission?
¿aceptan cheques de viajero?	do you take traveler's checks?

Travelling

quiero un boleto para Guadalajara	I'd like a ticket for Guadalajara	➤ Unit 4
un boleto de ida y vuelta	a round-trip ticket	➤ Unit 4
¿a qué hora sale?	what time does it leave?	➤ Unit 4
¿a qué hora llega?	what time does it arrive?	➤ Unit 4
está atrasado	it's late (delayed)	➤ Unit 4
¿qué tan atrasado está?	how late is it?	➤ Unit 4

In movie theaters, theaters, museums and galleries

quiero un boleto para esta función	I'd like a ticket for this showing	➤ Unit 4
¿a qué hora comienza?	what time does it begin?	➤ Unit 4
¿a qué hora termina?	what time does it end?	➤ Unit 4
¿a qué hora abre?	what time does it open?	➤ Unit 4
¿a qué hora cierra?	what time does it close?	➤ Unit 4
¿hay descuento?	is there a discount?	➤ Unit 4

In stores, restaurants, and cafés

quiero …	I would like …	➤ Unit 2
¿dónde puedo comprar …?	where can I buy …?	➤ Unit 6
tomo (esto) …	I'll have (this one) … (*literally* I'll take)	
¿cuánto es?	how much is it?	➤ Unit 2
¿algo más?	anything else?	➤ Unit 2/6
nada más	that'll be all (*literally* nothing else)	➤ Unit 2/6
¿aceptan tarjetas de crédito?	do you accept credit cards?	➤ Unit 2
¿puedo probármelo?	can I try it on?	➤ Unit 6
¿lo tiene en azul?	do you have it in blue?	➤ Unit 6
es (demasiado) grande/ pequeño	it's too big/small for me	➤ Unit 6
¡Disculpe!	excuse me! (*when calling the waiter*)	➤ Unit 2
queremos pedir	we'd like to order	
la carta, por favor	the menu, please	
el menú del día, por favor	the menu of the day, please	➤ Unit 2
¿qué quieren pedir?	what would you like to order?	➤ Unit 2
¿qué (me) recomienda?	what would you recommend (to me)?	
¿me puede traer [un vaso]?	could you please bring me [a glass]?	
un tenedor	a fork	
un cuchillo	a knife	
una cuchara	a spoon	
una servilleta	a napkin	
¿nos puede traer más [agua], por favor?	could we please have more [water]?	
pan	bread	
vino	wine	
la cuenta, por favor	the check, please	➤ Unit 2
junto/separado	together/separately	
pagar	to pay	
servicio incluido	service included	
quédese con el cambio	keep the change	
plato especial del día	today's special	
¿les ha gustado la comida?	did you enjoy your meal?	
(estuvo) muy buena	(it was) very good	
salud	cheers	
soy vegetariano/a	I'm vegetarian	
no como carne	I don't eat meat	
tengo alergia a …	I'm allergic to …	
esto no es para mí	this isn't for me	➤ Unit 2
no pedí esto	I didn't order this	
la cuenta está equivocada	the check is wrong	
no tomé eso	I didn't have that	

Menu reader

poco hecho	underdone (*meat*)	
medio hecho	medium cooked (*meat*)	
bien hecho	well done (*meat*)	
frito/a	fried (*masculine/feminine*)	
hervido/a, cocido/a	boiled	
a la plancha	grilled	
a la parrilla	grilled	
asado/a	roast(ed)	
asado/a	baked	
Bebidas	*Drinks*	
el agua mineral	mineral water	➤ Unit 2
con gas/sin gas	sparkling/still	➤ Unit 2
el agua de limón	water with lemon	➤ Unit 2
el jugo de naranja	orange juice	
el jugo de manzana	apple juice	
la malteada (de fresa)	(strawberry) milk shake	
una coca (cola)	Coca-Cola®, Coke®	
el hielo	ice	
el vino tinto	red wine	
el vino blanco	white wine	
el refresco	soda	
seco	dry	
(vino) de la casa	house (wine)	
la cerveza	beer	➤ Unit 2
el café americano	large black coffee	➤ Unit 2
el descafeinado	decaffeinated coffee	
el té negro	black tea	
el azúcar	sugar	
la leche	milk	
Primer Plato/Entradas	*Appetizers*	➤ Unit 2
la sopa	soup	➤ Unit 2
el caldo	meat and vegetable broth	
la ensalada	salad	➤ Unit 2
el jugo de tomate	tomato juice	
Segundo plato/Plato fuerte	*Main courses*	
Carnes	*Meat*	
(la carne de) res (*f*)	beef	
la ternera	veal	
la carne de cerdo	pork	
el lomo	pork loin	
el conejo	rabbit	

el cordero	lamb	
la chuleta de cordero	lamb chop	
la parrillada	mixed grill	
el pollo	chicken	
el pollo asado	roast chicken	➤ Unit 2
el pavo	turkey	
la salchicha	sausage	
el guisado	meat stew	
la machaca	ground or minced meat fried	

Pescados y Mariscos	*Fish and seafood*	➤ Unit 2
la mojarra	type of sea bream	
los calamares	squid	
los mejillones	mussels	
el huachinango	red snapper	
el atún	tuna	
la sardina	sardine	
la anchoa	anchovy	
los camarones	shrimps	
la langosta	lobster	

Verduras y Guarnición	*Vegetables and side dishes*
el espárrago	asparagus
la berenjena	eggplant, aubergine
los frijoles	beans
los garbanzos	garbanzo beans, chick peas
el col	cabbage
la zanahoria	carrot
la coliflor	cauliflower
la calabacita	zucchini, courgette
el pepino	cucumber
el ajo	garlic
el pepinillo	gherkin
las lentejas	lentils
los chícharos	peas
los hongos	mushrooms
la cebolla	onion
el pimiento rojo/verde	red/green pepper
el maíz	maize, corn
el tomate	tomato
la papa	potato
las papas fritas	(French) fries, chips; *also* chips, crisps
el arroz	rice
la pasta	noodles, pasta
el pan	bread

el huevo	egg
la sal	salt
la pimienta	pepper
el aceite	oil
el vinagre	vinegar
la mayonesa	mayonnaise
la mostaza	mustard

Botana	*Snacks*	➤ Unit 2
el taco	grilled meat wrapped in a warm tortilla topped with guacamole or other sauces	
la enchilada	corn tortilla filled with meat or chicken and enchilada sauce, topped with cheese	
la quesadilla	tortilla filled with a savory mixture and topped with melted cheese	
la tostada	deep-fried tortilla with vegetables, cheese and meat	
el guacamole	guacamole	
la torta de jamón	ham sandwich	
la torta de queso	cheese sandwich	
la torta de chorizo	spicy sausage sandwich	
el hot dog	hot dog	
la hamburguesa	hamburger	
el omelet	omelette	➤ Unit 2
la tortilla	corn or wheat flour tortilla	

Postres	*Desserts*	➤ Unit 2
el helado	ice cream	
el coctel de frutas	fruit salad	
la crema chantilly	whipped cream	
la fruta del tiempo	fresh fruit	
el flan	crème caramel	

Frutas y Frutos Secos	*Fruit and nuts*		
la manzana	apple	los cacahuates	peanuts
el chabacano	apricot	la pera	pear
la guayaba	guava	la ciruela	plum
el limón	lemon	la fresa	strawberry
la naranja	orange	la uva	grape
el durazno	peach	el zapote	sapodilla plum
el mango	mango	la nuez	walnut
la piña	pineapple		

What time of the day?

la mañana	morning	la tarde	evening (*early*)
la tarde	afternoon	la noche	night, late evening

When?

hoy	today	ahorita mismo	right now
mañana	tomorrow	pronto	soon
ayer	yesterday	el fin de semana	the weekend
esta noche	tonight	la próxima semana	next week
mañana por la noche	tomorrow night	la semana que viene	next week
ahorita	now		

Telling the time

¿qué hora es?	what time is it?
son las nueve	it's nine o'clock
son las nueve y media	it's nine thirty
son cuarto para las diez	it's a quarter to ten
son cinco para la diez	it's five to ten
son las diez y cuarto	it's a quarter after ten
son las diez y cinco	it's five after ten
es la una	it's one o'clock
vamos tarde	we're late
llegamos demasiado temprano	we're too early
comienza a las ocho	it begins at eight o'clock
termina a las ocho	it ends at eight o'clock
abre a las ocho	it opens at eight o'clock
cierra a las ocho	it closes at eight o'clock

What's the weather like?

¿como está el clima?	what's the weather like?	hace frío	it's cold
llueve/está lloviendo	it's raining	hace viento	it's windy
hace calor	it's hot/warm	nieva	it's snowing

How I feel

tengo sed	I'm thirsty	estoy enfermo/a	I'm ill
tengo hambre	I'm hungry	me duele la cabeza	I have a headache
estoy cansado/a	I'm tired	me duele la muela	I have a toothache
tengo sueño	I'm tired	tengo fiebre	I have a temperature
estoy mal	I feel ill	me duele la garganta	I have a bad throat
me encuentro mal	I feel ill	estoy mareado/a	I feel faint

Emergencies

llame a una ambulancia, por favor	call an ambulance, please
llame a la policía, por favor	call the police, please
¿me puede ayudar?	can you help me?
necesito un médico	I need a doctor
necesito un dentista	I need a dentist
busco una farmacia	I'm looking for a pharmacy

Directions

¿hay un banco por aquí?	is there a bank in the area?	➤ Unit 3
¿dónde está …?	where is …?	➤ Unit 3
¿en qué calle está …?	which street is …on?	
cerca de aquí	close by	➤ Unit 3
lejos de aquí	far from here	➤ Unit 3
no muy lejos de aquí	not far from here	
está a cinco minutos (de aquí)	it's five minutes (from here)	➤ Unit 3
a la derecha	on the right (hand side)	➤ Unit 3
a la izquierda	on the left (hand side)	➤ Unit 3
la derecha	right	➤ Unit 3
la izquierda	left	➤ Unit 3
todo derecho	right ahead	➤ Unit 3
hasta el final	to the end	➤ Unit 3
el semáforo	traffic lights	➤ Unit 3
la esquina	the corner	

Prepositions

al lado de	next to	➤ Unit 3
en	in, at, on	
encima de	on (top of)	
sobre	above/on	
detrás de	behind	
delante de	in front of, before	
enfrente (de)	opposite (to)	➤ Unit 3
entre	between	➤ Unit 3

What is it like and how does it look?

es (demasiado) grande	it's too big	
es (demasiado) pequeño/a	it's too small	➤ Unit 6
me queda bien	it fits	
es bonito/a	it's pretty	
me gusta	I like it	

verde	green	negro	black
rojo	red	blanco	white
azul	blue	morado	purple
café	brown	naranja	orange
amarillo	yellow	rosa	pink

Days of the week ➤ Unit 3

lunes	Monday	viernes	Friday
martes	Tuesday	sábado	Saturday
miércoles	Wednesday	domingo	Sunday
jueves	Thursday	el fin de semana	weekend

Months of the year ➤ Unit 4

enero	January	julio	July
febrero	February	agosto	August
marzo	March	septiembre	September
abril	April	octubre	October
mayo	May	noviembre	November
junio	June	diciembre	December

Numbers ➤ Units 2 and 3

1	uno	17	diecisiete	40	cuarenta
2	dos	18	dieciocho	43	cuarenta y tres
3	tres	19	diecinueve	50	cincuenta
4	cuatro	20	veinte	54	cincuenta y cuatro
5	cinco	21	veintiuno	60	sesenta
6	seis	22	veintidós	65	sesenta y cinco
7	siete	23	veintitrés	70	setenta
8	ocho	24	veinticuatro	76	setenta y seis
9	nueve	25	veinticinco	80	ochenta
10	diez	26	veintiséis	87	ochenta y siete
11	once	27	veintisiete	90	noventa
12	doce	28	veintiocho	98	noventa y ocho
13	trece	29	veintinueve	100	cien
14	catorce	30	treinta	101	ciento uno
15	quince	31	treinta y uno	200	doscientos
16	dieciséis	32	treinta y dos	250	doscientos cincuenta

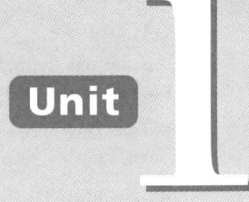

Greetings

In this unit you will learn how to :

- greet people
- introduce yourself
- ask how someone is
- say where you are from
- say where you live and where you work

Spanish is a relatively easy language to learn in the early stages because many words are similar to their English equivalents. When listening to the dialogues, listen out for words that sound familiar.

ACTIVITY 1 is on the recording.

DIALOGUE 1.1

■ Buenos días, señora García.

● Buenos días, señor Pérez, ¿cómo está?

■ Buenas tardes, señora Domínguez.

◆ Buenas tardes, José, ¿qué tal?

★ Buenas noches, señor Casas.

◆ ¡Ah! Señora Ruiz, buenas noches.

VOCABULARY

buenos días	good morning (*literally* good days)
señora	Mrs, Ms
¿cómo está?	how are you? (*formal*)
buenas tardes	good afternoon/evening (*literally* good afternoons/evenings)
señor	Mr
¿qué tal?	hi there, how are you doing? (*informal*)
buenas noches	goodnight (*literally* good nights)

● The equivalents of *good morning*, *good afternoon/evening*, and *goodnight* use the plural* form in Spanish (**buenos días** – literally *good days*, **buenas tardes** – *good afternoons/evenings*, **buenas noches** – *good nights*). Note that it is **bueno<u>s</u> días**, but **buena<u>s</u> tardes** and **buena<u>s</u> noches**. For the moment, learn these as set expressions. We will look at masculine* and feminine* agreement between words later in the course.

● **Buenos días** is used until lunchtime, **buenas tardes** for the afternoon and evening until about 9pm, after which **buenas noches** is used to greet and also to say *goodnight*. **Adiós** (*goodbye*) is also used to greet people if you pass them in the street and are not stopping.

● **¿Qué tal?** is the informal equivalent of *how are you?* and **¿cómo está?** the formal version. Note the use of **¿...?** to indicate a question. Spanish adopts the same system for exclamation marks: **¡...!: ¡Estupendo!** (*Fantastic!*)

ACTIVITY 2

Read dialogue 1.1 again and decide whether the statements below are true or false.

1. Señora García meets señor Pérez in the morning.   T/F
2. When José and señora Domínguez meet, José speaks first.   T/F
3. Señora Domínguez greets José informally.   T/F
4. Señor Casas and señora Ruiz are speaking in the afternoon.   T/F
5. We don't know if señor Casas and señora Ruiz are meeting
   each other or saying goodnight.   T/F

ACTIVITY 3

Now listen to the recording. At what time of day are the people meeting in each of the three dialogues?

any time		afternoon	
morning		night	

ACTIVITY 4

Number each of these six greetings from the recording as you hear each one. They are in a different order.

a. Buenas tardes.
b. Buenas tardes, Juan, ¿qué tal?
c. Buenos días, señor.
d. Buenos días.
e. Buenas noches, señora.
f. Buenas noches, Ana. ¿Cómo está?

ACTIVITIES 5 and 6 are on the recording.

ACTIVITY 7 is on the recording.

DIALOGUE 1.2

- Buenos días, me llamo Campos. ¿Cómo se llama usted?
- Me llamo Domínguez, Ana Domínguez.
- Mucho gusto.
- Mucho gusto, adiós.

- Hola, me llamo Carlos. ¿Cómo te llamas?
- Me llamo Javier. ¿Qué tal?
- Bien.
- Hasta luego.

VOCABULARY

me llamo	my name is (*literally* I call myself)
¿cómo se llama (usted)?	what's your name? (*formal*)
mucho gusto	pleased to meet you
hola	hello
adiós	goodbye
¿cómo te llamas?	what's your name? (*informal*)
bien	well, fine, OK
hasta luego	see you later

• There are two forms of address in Spanish; the informal **tú** and the more formal **usted**. The **tú** form is widely used amongst people of similar age and status, even when meeting for the first time. In stores, restaurants, banks and similar formal business situations, **usted** is normally used. If in doubt, use the **usted** form. So, if you ask someone formally for their name, say **¿Cómo se llama (usted)?** and if you are asking someone informally, for example at a party with people of your own age, say **¿Cómo te llamas (tú)?** The verb **llamarse** looks like this:

(yo) me llamo (*I am called*)   **(tú) te llamas** (*you are called*)
(él/ella/usted) se llama (*he/she is called, you* [formal] *are called*)

• Note that the subject pronouns* (**yo** – *I*, **tú** – *you*, **él** – *he*, **ella** – *she*, **usted** – *you* formal) are normally only used for emphasis and are not necessary in standard speech.

ACTIVITY 8

Listen to the recording and complete these dialogues. Or try to fill the gaps before listening, then check your answers.

- Buenas _____ , _____ llamo García, Fernando García. ¿Cómo _____ _____ usted?

- Mucho _____ . Yo me _____ Ana Ruiz.

- Mucho _____ , adiós.

- Hola, me llamo Carlos. ¿Cómo te _____ ?

- Me _____ Fernando. ¿Qué _____ ?

- Bien. Hasta _____ .

ACTIVITY 9

Find the two dialogues from the jumbled lines below. One is formal and the other informal.

Me llamo Rosa. ¿Cómo te llamas tú?
Buenos días. Me llamo Francisco González. ¿Cómo se llama usted?
Hola, ¿qué tal? ¿Cómo te llamas?
Me llamo Daniel.
Hasta luego.
Mucho gusto. Adiós.
Me llamo Javier Martín.
Mucho gusto.

ACTIVITIES 10 and 11 are on the recording.

ACTIVITY 12 is on the recording.

DIALOGUE 1.3

- Buenos días; me llamo Andrés Sánchez. ¿Cómo te llamas?
- Me llamo Pedro Pérez. Soy de Guadalajara. ¿Y tú? ¿de dónde eres?
- Soy de la Ciudad de México pero vivo en Monterrey.
- Buenos días. Me llamo Martínez, Pilar Martínez. ¿Cómo se llama usted?
- Me llamo Pedro Pérez. ¿De dónde es usted, Señora Martínez?
- Soy de Guadalajara; ¿y usted? ¿de dónde es?
- Yo también soy de Guadalajara. Pero trabajo en Puebla.

VOCABULARY	
soy de Guadalajara (verb **ser**)	I am from Guadalajara (to be)
¿y tú?	and you?
¿de dónde eres?	where are you from?
pero	but
vivo (verb **vivir**)	I live (to live)
¿de dónde es (usted)?	where are you from? (*formal*)
yo	I
también	also
trabajo (verb **trabajar**)	I work (to work)
en	in

- There are three types of regular verbs, those ending in **-ar** (**trabajar** – *to work*), those ending in **-er** (**comer** – *to eat*), and those ending in **-ir** (**vivir** – *to live*).

(yo) trabajo – I work	**(nosotros/as) trabaj**amos – we work
(tú) trabajas – you work	**(ustedes) trabaj**an – you work
(él/ella) trabaja – he/she/it works	**(ellos/ellas) trabaj**an – they work
(usted) trabaja – you work (*formal*)	
(yo) vivo – I live	**(nosotros/as) viv**imos – we live
(tú) vives – you live	**(ustedes) viv**en – you live
(él/ella) vive – he/she/it lives	**(ellos/ellas) viv**en – they live
(usted) vive – you live (*formal*)	

(yo) como – I eat   **(nosotros/as) comemos** – we eat
(tú) comes – you eat   **(ustedes) comen** – you eat
(él/ella) come – he/she/it eats   **(ellos/ellas) comen** – they eat
(usted) come – you eat (*formal*)

● The verb **ser** (*to be*) is irregular and is conjugated as follows:

(yo) soy – I am   **(nosotros/as) somos** – we are
(tú) eres – you are   **(ustedes) son** – you are
(él/ella) es – he/she/it is   **(ellos/ellas) son** – they are
(usted) es – you are (*formal*)

● There are several ways of asking questions. One is by using a question word like
¿Dónde …? (where?) or **¿De dónde …?** (*literally* from where …?).

ACTIVITY 13

Here are the names of the three speakers from dialogue 1.3:
Andrés Sánchez, Pedro Pérez, Pilar Martínez

1. Who is from Guadalajara?
2. Who works in Puebla?
3. Who lives in Monterrey?
4. Who is from Mexico City?

ACTIVITY 14

Complete these sentences, using the correct form of ser (soy, eres, or es).

1. (Yo) _____ de Guadalajara.
2. ¿(Tú) _____ de la Ciudad de México?
3. ¿De dónde _____ (usted)?
4. La señora Yuste _____ de Zacatecas.
5. El señor Caspe _____ de Aguascalientes.

 ACTIVITIES 15 and **16** are on the recording.

ACTIVITY 17 is on the recording.

DIALOGUE 1.4

- ¿De dónde es usted?
- Soy de Inglaterra, ¿y usted?
- Soy de Estados Unidos. Soy estadounidense.

- ¿Eres inglesa?
- No, soy australiana. ¿Y tú?, ¿de dónde eres?
- Soy de México. Soy mexicano.

VOCABULARY

Inglaterra	England
los Estados Unidos	the United States
estadounidense	American (from the United States)
inglés/inglesa	English
australiano/a	Australian
México	Mexico
mexicano/a	Mexican

- There are two ways to state your nationality:
1. with the phrase **soy de** + the name of the country (**soy de los Estados Unidos** – *I am from the United States*; **soy de México** – *I am from Mexico*.)
2. with **soy** + the appropriate nationality adjective* (**soy inglés** – *I am English* [male]; **soy inglesa** – *I am English* [female]).
Note that nationality adjectives always begin with a lower case letter (**mexicano**, **australiana**) whereas countries always begin with a capital letter (**México**, **Australia**). Like all adjectives, nationality adjectives agree with the person or persons they are describing, so their endings vary: **mexicano** to describe one male, **mexicana** for one female, **mexicanos** for two or more people including at least one male, and **mexicanas** for two or more females.
- Most Spanish words are stressed on the *penultimate* syllable* (**Inglaterra**, **inglesa**). Words ending in a consonant* (except **n** or **s**) are automatically stressed on the *last* syllable (**Madrid**, **usted**). Words which do not follow these rules of stress have a written accent on the stressed syllable (**inglés**, **también**, **Domínguez**, **adiós**, **América**). Make sure you stress the appropriate syllable.

ACTIVITY 18

Here is a mixture of countries and nationalities. Make three lists, one for the countries, one for male nationality, and one for female nationality. Some are not so clear, so you'll have to do some guesswork.

portugués Italia brasileño Turquía Argentina Portugal griego argentina Francia Irlanda peruano alemán francesa Japón italiana irlandés estadounidense Brasil japonesa Estados Unidos Alemania turco Perú Grecia

ACTIVITY 19

Here are some questions and answers about nationality. Complete either the question or the answer as indicated, remembering to use the **tú** form or the **usted** form for the questions as indicated.

Example: **¿De dónde eres?**   **Soy inglés.**

1. ¿ _____ (usted)?   _____ Estados Unidos.

2. ¿ _____ (tú) argentino?   Sí, _____ Argentina.

3. ¿ _____ (usted) de Estados Unidos? No. _____ inglesa.

4. ¿De dónde _____ (tú)?   _____ australiana.

ACTIVITY 20

Pronounce the following words with the correct stress, according to the rules described above. Then listen to them on the recording.

señora, Pérez, noche, también, adiós, usted, México, inglesa, inglés, español

ACTIVITY 21 is on the recording.

Culture

Some facts about Mexico and Mexican life and people.

In Mexico, people don't say **por favor** (*please*), **gracias** (*thank you*) and **disculpe** (*excuse me*) nearly as much as in the U.S. Spoken Spanish is a much more direct language than English and so its speakers themselves sound more direct.

In Spanish conversation, it is quite normal for a group of people to all speak loudly and at the same time as each other in order to get their point across. They may appear to be interrupting each other. Spanish speakers are great conversationalists and bars, buses, trains, markets and streets are full of people engaged in animated conversation. They speak as much with their hands and arms as with their tongues.

When meeting Latin Americans, be prepared to shake hands more than you might in the U.S., as this is the normal form of formal greeting. You may also be aware of a greater degree of formality in business meetings or exchanges.

Family members or very close friends usually kiss each other on the right cheek when they meet and when they say goodbye. It is also common to see adult men, who are good friends or family, embracing when they meet. In general Latin Americans are more physical when it comes to greetings and farewells and you will see a greater degree of physical contact.

The Latin goodbye. One thing that Latin Americans are not very direct about is taking their leave. In social circles, getting up to go does not mean that the party is over. It is quite common for people to announce they are leaving, only to be found still talking at the door a good while later. The conversation may well continue out into the street. Get used to the culture shock of long goodbyes! Useful expressions when taking your leave are **hasta luego** (literally *until later*, but used in the same way as *see you around*); **hasta mañana** (*see you tomorrow*), and **nos vemos luego/mañana** (*we'll see each other later/tomorrow*)

A typical working day in Mexico depends on whether you work for the public or private sector. The official working day laid down by the government for public sector workers involves a morning's work from about 9.00 until 2.00 and then again from 4.00 until 8.00, with a two-hour lunch break in the middle of the day. Most people live too far away to go home for lunch during this period and so have lunch near their place of work. Workers in the private sector work from 9.00 until 2.00 and then only have one hour for lunch before beginning again at 3.00 and working until 7.00. Stores also close around 7 or 8 in the evening. In the larger towns, especially Mexico City which covers a very large area, it often takes workers more than an hour to travel to work and the same to return home again, so try to avoid periods of the day when the public transport system is very busy.

Review 1

1. Match the Spanish phrase with the English equivalent.

1. Me llamo	a. Goodbye!
2. ¿De dónde es usted?	b. How are you? (*formal*)
3. ¡Adiós!	c. I live in …
4. Soy de …	d. Where are you from?
5. ¿Cómo está?	e. I am from …
6. Buenas tardes	f. How are you? (*informal*)
7. Vivo en …	g. My name is …
8. ¿Qué tal?	h. Good evening!

2. Write down what the following people would say about themselves.

Name:	Ana Martínez	John Adams	Jane Smith
Nationality:	Mexican	Australian	American
comes from:	Mexico City	Sydney	Boston
lives in:	Mexico City	London	Chicago
works in:	Mexico City	London	Chicago

3. These sentences are in the wrong order. Put them in the correct order to make a conversation.

a. Me llamo Ana Duarte.

b. Buenos días, señora Duarte.

c. Soy de Guadalajara.

d. Yo también soy de Guadalajara, pero vivo en Monterrey.

e. ¿De dónde es usted?

Time to Listen

4. Listen to the conversation on the recording and fill in the gaps.

Buenos _____ , señora García.

_____ , señor Pérez, ¿ _____ usted?

Muy bien, gracias. Éste _____ Pedro González.

Hola, Pedro. _____ gusto. ¿De _____ eres?

_____ de Guadalajara, pero _____ en la Ciudad de México.

Yo también _____ en la Ciudad de México.

5. Listen to these questions and indicate whether the speakers are using the formal or the informal form.

1. formal/informal
2. formal/informal
3. formal/informal
4. formal/informal
5. formal/informal
6. formal/informal
7. formal/informal

6. Listen to people introducing themselves and giving their nationality. Link each name with the correct country.

Patrick	**Escocia**
John	**Irlanda**
Isobel	**Inglaterra**
Clark	**Australia**
Jane	**Estados Unidos**

Time to talk

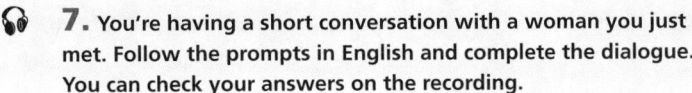

7. You're having a short conversation with a woman you just met. Follow the prompts in English and complete the dialogue. You can check your answers on the recording.

Buenas tardes.
(Say good afternoon and then ask her for her name.)
Me llamo Rosa Martínez. ¿Cómo se llama usted?
(Say your name is Tom Jones.)
(Ask where she is from.)
Soy de la Ciudad de México, pero vivo en Guadalajara; ¿y usted?, ¿de dónde es?
(Tell her you are from from Boston, but you live in New York.)

Now do the same dialogue addressing the woman informally.

8. Test your progress in Unit 1. How would you …?

a. greet someone in the morning
b. greet someone in the early evening
c. ask someone where they come from (*formally and informally*)
d. say that you come from the United States
e. say 'how are you?' (*formally and informally*)
f. say 'see you later'
g. tell someone where you live
h. tell someone where you work
i. say 'pleased to meet you'

You can check your answers on the recording.

In a bar or restaurant

In this unit you will learn how to:

- order food and drink
- ask what there is on the menu
- ask for the check
- count up to 50

Don't worry about getting things wrong. Even if you make mistakes people will still be able to understand you. The more confidence you gain through communicating, the more fluent you will become.

ACTIVITY 1 is on the recording.

DIALOGUE 2.1

- Buenos días.
- Buenos días. Quiero café americano, por favor. ¿Quieres café americano?
- No. Para mí, agua.
- ¿Agua de limón?
- Sí, agua de limón.
- ¿Algo más?
- No. Nada más. ¿Cuánto es?
- Son treinta pesos.

VOCABULARY

quiero, quieres (verb querer)	I want/I'd like, you want (to want)
el café americano	large black offee
por favor	please
para mí	for me
un agua (f)	a glass of water
el agua de limón	water with lemon
¿algo más?	anything else?
nada más	nothing else
¿cuánto es?	how much is it?
son treinta pesos	that's 30 pesos
	(*literally* they are 30 pesos)

- **Querer** (*to want*) is often used as the equivalent of *would like*, as in **quiero café americano** (*I'd like a black coffee*). When inviting someone to drink or eat something, say: **¿quieres café americano?** (*would you like black coffee?*) to a friend or family member, or **¿quiere café americano?** in a more formal situation. Note the insertion of the letter **i** after the letter **u** which changes pronunciation – **(yo) quiero** (*I want, I'd like*), **(tú) quieres** (*you want*), **(él/ella/usted) quiere** (*he/she/you want(s)*). By adding **no** before **quiero** you can say *I don't want* (**no quiero**).

● Note that the reply to the question **¿cuánto es?** (*how much is it?*) is **son treinta pesos** (literally *they are thirty pesos*).

ACTIVITY 2

Read dialogue 2.1 again and decide whether each of the following statements is true or false:

1. They are in the bar in the afternoon.   T/F
2. Both customers want a drink.   T/F
3. They don't want anything else.   T/F
4. One of the customers wants water with lemon.   T/F
5. The check is more than thirty pesos.   T/F

ACTIVITY 3

Match the Spanish sentences with the English. Add question marks where necessary.

1. **buenos días**   a. for me
2. **nada más**   b. anything else?
3. **algo más**   c. how much is it?
4. **quiero**   d. I'd like
5. **para mí**   e. nothing else
6. **cuánto es**   f. good morning

ACTIVITIES 4 and **5** are on the recording.

ACTIVITY 6 is on the recording.

DIALOGUE 2.2

■ Hola, buenas tardes. ¿Qué quieren ustedes?

▨ Buenas tardes. Quiero café americano, por favor.

● Y para mí, una coca.

■ Muy bien. ¿Quieren botana?

● Sí, yo quiero guacamole.

▨ Para mí unas quesadillas.

   […]

■ Aquí tiene.

▨ Gracias. ¿Cuánto es?

■ Son cincuenta pesos.

VOCABULARY

¿qué quieren ustedes?	what would you like? (*plural*)
y	and
muy bien	OK (*literally* very well)
la coca	Coca-Cola®
¿quieren …?	would you like …? (*plural*)
la botana	bar snack
sí	yes
el guacamole	guacamole
la quesadilla	snack of filled tortilla
aquí tiene	here you are (*literally* here you have it)
gracias	thank you
cincuenta pesos	fifty pesos

● To ask a question starting with *what*, add **¿qué …?** before the verb*: **¿Qué quieren ustedes?** (*What would you like?*).

● All Spanish nouns* are either masculine* or feminine*. Masculine nouns often end in **-o** and feminine nouns in **-a**, but many do not follow this rule and must be learned individually. The equivalent of *a* and *an* in English is **un** for masculine and **una** for feminine singular, as in **un café americano** (*a large black coffee*), **una coca** (*a cola*).

● Here are the Spanish numbers from 0–20, followed by a selection of numbers from 25 to 50. They are also on the recording.

0 cero

1 uno	6 seis	11 once	16 dieciséis
2 dos	7 siete	12 doce	17 diecisiete
3 tres	8 ocho	13 trece	18 dieciocho
4 cuatro	9 nueve	14 catorce	19 diecinueve
5 cinco	10 diez	15 quince	20 veinte
25 veinticinco	30 treinta	35 treinta y cinco	40 cuarenta
45 cuarenta y cinco	50 cincuenta		

ACTIVITY 7

Match the items below. Can you guess the ones you haven't learned yet?

1. **un café americano**
2. **una coca**
3. **un agua mineral**
4. **un agua de limón**

a. mineral water
b. water with lemon
c. black coffee
d. cola

ACTIVITY 8

Look at these prices and write them in words. Make sure you start each one with **Son** ... Here is an example: 25 pesos – **Son veinticinco pesos.**

a. 35 pesos
b. 20 pesos
c. 15 pesos
d. 45 pesos
e. 50 pesos
f. 12 pesos

 ACTIVITIES 9 and **10** are on the recording.

ACTIVITY 11 is on the recording.

DIALOGUE 2.3

- Buenos días. ¿Qué van a comer?
- El menú del día, por favor.
- Muy bien. Para empezar hay ensalada o sopa.
- Para mí, ensalada.
- Y yo quiero sopa.
- Muy bien. Luego hay pollo o pescado.
- Para mí, pollo.
- Y para mí, pescado.
- ¿Para beber?
- Cerveza y agua de limón.

VOCABULARY

¿qué van a comer?	what will you have?
el menú del día	menu of the day (*cheap set daily special*)
para empezar	to begin (*for the first course*)
hay	there is/there are
la ensalada	salad
la sopa	soup
luego	then (*for the main course*)
el pollo	chicken
el pescado	fish
para beber	to drink
la cerveza	beer

- In Spanish, **el** and **la** both mean *the*, **el** being used with masculine* words and **la** with feminine*. The plurals* are **los** and **las**. Here are some examples: **el café** (*the coffee*), **la sopa** (*the soup*), **los pollos** (*the chickens*), **las cervezas** (*the beers*). Note that **agua** (*the water*), a feminine word, uses the masculine definite article* (**el agua**).

• **hay** (*there is/there are*) is a simple and versatile word. The question form and the negative* form are as follows: **¿hay …?** (*is there?/are there?*), **¿qué hay?** (*what is there?*), **no hay** (*there isn't/there aren't*). Look at these examples:

¿Hay quesadillas?	**Sí, hay.**
¿Hay agua?	**No, no hay.**
¿Qué hay?	**Hay quesadillas.**

ACTIVITY 12

Read dialogue 2.3 again, and answer the following questions by selecting the correct response from the list below.

a. fish
b. salad
c. salad or soup

d. beer and water with lemon
e. chicken
f. soup

1. What does the waiter offer for the first course?
2. What does the man order for the first course?
3. What does the woman order for the first course?
4. What does the man order for the main course?
5. What does the woman order for the main course?
6. What do they order to drink?

ACTIVITY 13

Ask what's available in the bar, using **¿Hay …?** and any of the items from the list. Answer using the prompts next to each item.

Example: **¿Hay agua? Sí, hay.**

menú del día ✓   pollo ✓
ensalada ✓   pescado ✗
sopa ✗   cerveza ✓

 ACTIVITIES 14 and **15** are on the recording.

ACTIVITY 16 is on the recording.

DIALOGUE 2.4

- ¿Quieren postre?
- ¿Qué hay?
- Hay helado y flan.
- No quiero postre. Yo quiero un té negro.
- Y yo, un café americano.
  […]
- Aquí tienen ... Dos cafés americanos.
- No. El café americano no es para mí. Quiero un té negro.
- Perdone. Ahorita lo traigo.
- Y la cuenta, por favor. ¿Aceptan tarjetas de crédito?
- Sí, señor.

VOCABULARY

el postre	dessert
¿qué hay?	what is there?
el helado	ice cream
el flan	crème caramel
el té negro	black tea
no es para mí	it isn't for me
perdone	I'm sorry
ahorita lo traigo	I'll bring it right away
la cuenta	the check
¿aceptan? (verb aceptar)	do you take? (*literally* to accept)
la tarjeta de crédito	credit card

- Note that the equivalents of *I*, *you*, *he/she*, etc. (the subject pronouns*) are usually omitted in general speech because the ending of the verb itself tells us which person is being referred to. The subject pronouns are as follows:
yo (*I*), **tú** (*you*), **él** (*he*), **ella** (*she*), **usted** (*you* singular formal), **nosotros/nosotras** (*we*), **ustedes** (*you* plural), **ellos/ellas** (*they*).

They are normally used for emphasis as in this example
- **¿Qué quieres beber?** (*What do you want to drink?*)
- **Quiero una cerveza.** (*I'd like a beer.*)
- **Yo quiero agua.** (*I would like water.*)

ACTIVITY 17

Read dialogue 2.4 again and write it in English. Try to do this without looking at the vocabulary.

ACTIVITY 18

Complete this dialogue by filling in the gaps with either **hay** or **quiero**.

A ¿Qué _____ para comer?

B _____ pollo y pescado.

A No _____ pollo. Yo _____ pescado.

C Y yo, pollo.

B … Aquí tienen … Dos pollos.

A No. El pollo no es para mí. _____ pescado.

B Perdone.

ACTIVITY 19

Write the following in Spanish using **hay**.

1. What is there?
2. Is there any ice cream?
3. There's chicken and fish.
4. There aren't any snacks.
5. There is ice cream.

ACTIVITIES 20 and **21** are on the recording.

Culture

The role of **la cafetería** and **el café** is important in the social and business life of Mexico and other Latin American countries. **Cafeterías** are like self-serve restaurants, with an informal atmosphere. They offer breakfast, lunch, or an evening meal, as well as other food and snacks, such as **tortas** (*a kind of sandwich*), throughout the day. Look out for **la comida corrida**, a cheap, fixed price meal of several courses, served at lunchtime. Order your drink and food at the bar and stay at the bar or find a table. **Cafeterías** are open until about 8 or 9 o'clock at night.

A **café** is more elegant than a **cafetería**, but does not normally sell alcohol. Wait at your table to be served by **el mesero** or **la mesera** (*waiter/waitress*). Ask for **la cuenta** (*the check*) when you want to pay. Leave **una propina** (*a tip*) of up to about 10%.

Los bares (*bars*) serve mainly alcoholic drinks. They open in the early evening and stay open until the early hours of the morning.

In bars, it is common for people to simply say the name of the drink, for example **una cerveza** (*a beer*), when they are at the bar, or to say **¿me da una cerveza?** (*give me a beer*). Be aware that if you patiently wait your turn at a bar without asserting yourself, you may not get served at all.

Coffee (**café**) is normally served black. There's usually a jug of milk (**la leche**) on the table. If you want tea, ask for **un té negro** (*a black tea*). If you just ask for **un té**, you'll probably be given a camomile tea.

Cerveza (*beer*) is very popular in Mexico, more so than wine. Mexico is also famous for its **tequila**. Coca Cola and Pepsi are widely available, as are local sodas, such as **refresco de naranja** (*orange soda*). **Aguas frescas**, fruit-based drinks with sugar, include **limonada** (*lemon soda*). **Jugos** (*juices*) such as **jugo de naranja** (*orange juice*) are also available.

Much of Mexico's 'cuisine' is based on three main items: **la tortilla**, a thin round pancake made from corn or wheat flour; **los frijoles** (*beans*); and various styles of **arroz** (*rice*).

El taco is a rolled tortilla filled with pieces of meat and beans. **La enchilada** is a corn tortilla filled with meat and topped with a special **salsa** (*sauce*). **La quesadilla** is a tortilla folded in half and filled with meat or vegetables. Quesadillas are usually fried.

ACTIVITY 22

Here are some items from a **comida corrida** or **menú del día**. Identify each item and separate each one into **primer plato** (*first course*), **segundo plato** (*main course*), **postre** (*dessert*) and **bebidas** (*drinks*). Then practice ordering from the menu you have created, using **quiero**, **para mí**, etc.

ensalada	pollo asado
sopa de frijoles	cerveza
jugo de tomate	enchilada
cerveza	helado
fruta del tiempo	café americano
agua	flan
refresco de naranja	pescado

Review 2

1. Match each phrase or question with its English equivalent.
Add question marks (¿...?) where appropriate.

1. para mí		**a.** here you are
2. algo más		**b.** how much is that?
3. no es para mí		**c.** thanks
4. nada más		**d.** please
5. cuánto es		**e.** for me
6. aquí tiene(n)		**f.** nothing else
7. por favor		**g.** anything else?
8. gracias		**h.** it isn't for me

2. Match these numbers with the corresponding words:

a. 20		**1.** nueve
b. 13		**2.** quince
c. 9		**3.** dieciocho
d. 18		**4.** trece
e. 35		**5.** veinticinco
f. 15		**6.** veinte
g. 12		**7.** doce
h. 25		**8.** treinta y cinco

3. Match the questions with the answers.

1. ¿quiere postre?		**a.** un agua de limón
2. ¿hay helado?		**b.** nada más
3. ¿qué van a comer?		**c.** son sesenta pesos
4. ¿qué hay?		**d.** no, no quiero
5. ¿para beber?		**e.** el menú del día
6. ¿aceptan Visa?		**f.** hay pollo y pescado
7. ¿algo más?		**g.** sí, claro
8. ¿cuánto es?		**h.** sí hay

Time to Listen

4. Listen to the conversation on the recording and complete what the customer says.

- Buenos días ¿Qué van a comer?
- _____
- Para empezar hay jugo de tomate o ensalada.
- _____
- Muy bien. ¿Y luego?
- _____
- ¿Para beber?
- _____

5. Listen to these ten numbers and write each one in the box as you hear it.

6. You will hear two people ordering from the bar. Indicate M for Man and W for Woman where relevant.

large black coffee		salad	
black tea		soup	
orange soda		fish	
water with lemon		crème caramel	
beer		fruit	
still water		ice cream	

Time to talk

7. You are ordering something in a bar. Follow the prompts in English and complete the dialogue. You can check your answers on the recording.

Buenas tardes, ¿qué quiere?
(Ask if they have snacks.)
Sí hay. ¿Quiere botana?
(Say yes and say you want a quesadilla.)
¿Y para beber?
(Ask for a beer.)
Aquí tiene.
(Say thank you and ask how much it is.)
Son treinta y cinco pesos.
(Say 'here you are'.)

8. Test your progress in Unit 2. How would you ...?

a. say you want a large black coffee
b. say 'for me, a water with lemon'
c. say you don't want anything else
d. ask how much it is
e. ask for the check
f. ask if there are any 'quesadillas'
g. ask what there is on the menu
h. say you don't want chicken
i. say numbers from 1 to 10
j. ask if they take credit cards

You can check your answers on the recording.

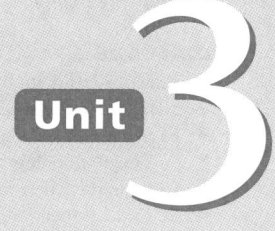

Directions

In this unit you will learn how to:

- ask for and follow simple street directions
- ask if something is nearby or far away
- explain where things are in relation to one another (next to, opposite, etc.)
- count up to 1000

Guesswork is an important part of learning a new language. In Spanish there are lots of words which are similar to English. Don't be afraid to guess the meanings of words in context – you'll be surprised how often you are right.

ACTIVITY 1 is on the recording.

DIALOGUE 3.1

- ■ Disculpe. ¿Hay un banco por aquí?
- ● Sí señor. Todo derecho, la primera calle a la derecha.
- ■ La primera calle a la derecha …
- ● Sí. Luego todo derecho y la segunda calle a la izquierda.
- ■ La segunda calle a la izquierda.
- ● Sí, hasta el final.
- ■ Muchas gracias.

VOCABULARY

disculpe	excuse me
el banco	bank
por aquí	around here
todo derecho	straight ahead
la primera calle	the first street
a la derecha	on the right
luego	then, afterwards
la segunda calle	the second street
a la izquierda	on the left
hasta el final	to the end (of the street)
muchas gracias	many thanks, thank you very much

● The Spanish words for *1st, 2nd, 3rd, 4th,* etc. (**primero, segundo, tercero, cuarto**), end in **-o** for masculine* and **-a** for feminine*. Look at these examples:

el primer banco (*the first bank*)   **la primera calle** (*the first street*)
el segundo bar (*the second bar*)   **la segunda cafetería** (*the second cafe*)
el tercer semáforo (*the third traffic lights*)   **la tercera casa** (*the third house*)
el cuarto edificio (*the fourth building*)   **la cuarta tienda** (*the fourth store*)

Note that the **-o** is omitted from **primero** and **tercero** in the masculine examples.

● Other services are: **el correo** (*post office*), **la oficina de cambio** (*currency exchange*), **la delegación de policía** (*police station*), **la oficina de turismo** (*tourist office*), **el hospital** (*hospital*), **la farmacia** (*pharmacy*).

ACTIVITY 2

Read dialogue 3.1 again and decide whether these statements are true or false:

1. He has to take the first on the right.   T/F
2. Then he has to go straight ahead.   T/F
3. He has to take the first on the left.   T/F
4. He has to go to the end of the street.   T/F

ACTIVITY 3

Here is a list of directions in English. On the recording you will hear them in Spanish in a different order. Number them in the order you hear them.

a. the first street on the left   b. the second street on the right
c. the third street on the left   d. straight ahead to the end of the street

ACTIVITY 4

Fill in the gaps by choosing the correct word from the list below:
calle   todo   calle   aqui   calle   la   hasta   hay   hasta   por

A: ¿ _____ un hospital _____ _____ ?
B: Sí. La segunda _____ a _____ izquierda. _____ derecho
     _____ el final. La primera _____ a la derecha. Todo derecho
     _____ el final de la _____ .

ACTIVITY 5

Write these in Spanish:

1. 1st street on the left.
2. 1st bank on the right.
3. 3rd street on the right.
4. Straight ahead, 2nd on the right, to the end of the street.

ACTIVITIES 6 and 7 are on the recording.

ACTIVITY 8 is on the recording.

DIALOGUE 3.2

- Disculpe. ¿Dónde está la catedral?
- La catedral está en el zócalo.
- ¿Está lejos?
- No. Está cerca. Está a cinco minutos de aquí.
- ¿A cinco minutos?
- Sí. Todo derecho. El zócalo está al final de la calle.
- Muchas gracias.
- De nada.

VOCABULARY

¿dónde está ...?	where is ...?
la catedral	cathedral
el zócalo	main square
¿está lejos?	is it far?
está cerca	it's not far (*literally* it's near)
a cinco minutos	five minutes away
de aquí	from here
al final	at the end
de nada	don't mention it/you're welcome

● The verb* **estar** is one of two verbs meaning *to be*. The other is **ser**, which you saw in Unit 1. **Estar** is used for location. For example, **la catedral está en la plaza** (*the cathedral is in the square*), or **está cerca** (*it's not far*). It is conjugated as follows:

estoy	**estás**	**está**	**estamos**	**están**
I am	*you are*	*he/she/it is*	*we are*	*you/they are*
		you are (singular formal)		

● Questions can be formed by changing the intonation of a statement. For example, **está lejos** (*it's a long way*) becomes **¿está lejos?** (*is it far?*). Listen to the example in the dialogue and in the pronunciation practice. Questions are also formed by adding a question word before the verb: **¿Dónde está?** (*Where is it?*).

● When you want to express how far away something is in time or distance, use **a** + the time or the distance. **Está a cinco minutos** (*It is five minutes away*, literally *it's at five minutes*), or **Está a diez kilómetros (de aquí)** (*It's ten kilometers from here*).

ACTIVITY 9

Here is a similar dialogue to dialogue 3.2, but it is jumbled up. Put it into the correct order.

¿Está cerca?
No. Está lejos. A quince minutos de aquí.
Sí. Todo derecho. La primera calle a la derecha. Hasta el final de la calle.
Disculpe, ¿Dónde está el correo?
El correo está en la avenida Goya.
De nada.
¿Quince minutos?
Gracias.

ACTIVITY 10

Write these sentences in Spanish:

1. Excuse me. Where is the police station?
2. Where is the bus station?
3. Is there a post office around here?
4. Is it far?
5. Go straight ahead to the end of the road.

ACTIVITIES 11 and **12** are on the recording.

ACTIVITY 13 is on the recording.

DIALOGUE 3.3

■ Disculpe. ¿Dónde está la oficina de turismo?

■ Está al final de la calle, al lado de la estación de autobuses.

■ ¿Dónde está la delegación de policía?

■ Está a cinco minutos, enfrente del parque.

■ ¿Hay una farmacia por aquí?

■ Sí hay. Tome la primera a la izquierda. Está entre el cine y la librería.

■ ¿Dónde está el museo?

■ Está muy lejos. Está en las afueras de la ciudad.

VOCABULARY	
al lado de	next to (*literally* at the side of)
enfrente de	opposite
el parque	park
tome (verb **tomar**)	take (to take)
entre	between
el cine	movie theater
la librería	bookstore
el museo	museum, gallery
muy	very
las afueras	the edge (of town)
la ciudad	city

Here are some words which tell you where things are located. They normally follow the verb* **estar: está detrás del banco** (*it's behind the bank*).

delante de (*in front of*), **detrás de** (*behind*), **debajo de** (*under*), **encima de** (*on top of, above*), **entre** (*between*) and **sobre** (*above, on*).

Note that **de + el = del**, as in **delante *del* parque** (*in front of the park*). The same thing happens with **a + el = al**, as in **al lado de** (*next to*), **al final** (*at/to the end*).

ACTIVITY 14

Read dialogue 3.3 again and complete the following:

1. The tourist office is
   a. behind the bus station b. next to the bus station
   c. opposite the bus station
2. The police station is
   a. opposite the park b. in front of the park c. next to the park
3. The movie theater is
   a. next to the bookstore b. next to the pharmacy
   c. opposite the pharmacy and the bookstore
4. The museum is
   a. downtown b. near here c. on the edge of town

ACTIVITY 15

Translate these sentences into Spanish.

1. The bookstore is next to the cathedral.
2. The post office is opposite the park.
3. The bus station is on the edge of town.
4. The tourist office is between the pharmacy and the movie theater.
5. The police station is a long way away.

ACTIVITY 16

Read these answers and write down the questions.

1. No. Está cerca.
2. La catedral está al final de la calle.
3. Sí, hay un correo.
4. No. La farmacia está al lado del cine, no enfrente.

ACTIVITIES 17 and 18 are on the recording.

ACTIVITY 19 is on the recording.

DIALOGUE 3.4

- Necesito ir a Querétaro. ¿Está cerca?
- Cerca no. Está a ciento sesenta y cinco kilómetros, al norte.
- También quiero visitar Puebla. ¿Está cerca?
- Sí. Está a ochenta kilómetros al este de la Ciudad de México.
- Y quiero viajar a Acapulco, también.
- Acapulco está lejos, a cuatrocientos sesenta kilómetros al sur de aquí.
- Quiero visitar Manzanillo. ¿Dónde está?
- Está a ochocientos kilómetros al oeste.

VOCABULARY	
necesito (verb **necesitar**)	I need (to need)
ir	to go
a	to
ciento sesenta y cinco	a hundred and sixty-five
al norte	to the north
también	also
visitar	to visit
ochenta	eighty
al este	to the east
viajar	to travel
cuatrocientos	four hundred
al sur	to the south
de	from, of
al oeste	to the west

- Numbers from 50. The tens are as follows: **cincuenta** (*50*) **sesenta** (*60*) **setenta** (*70*) **ochenta** (*80*) **noventa** (*90*).
The hundreds are as follows: **cien** (*100*) **doscientos** (*200*) **trescientos** (*300*) **cuatrocientos** (*400*) **quinientos** (*500*) **seiscientos** (*600*) **setecientos** (*700*) **ochocientos** (*800*) **novecientos** (*900*) **mil** (*1000*).

Note the difference between the 20s and the 30s to 90s: **veintiuno** (*21*) **veintidós** (*22*) **veintitrés** (*23*) **veinticuatro** (*24*) **veinticinco** (*25*) **veintiséis** (*26*) **veintisiete** (*27*) **veintiocho** (*28*) **veintinueve** (*29*) **treinta** (*30*) **treinta y uno** (*31*) **treinta y dos** (*32*) **treinta y tres** (*33*) **cuarenta y cuatro** (*44*) **cincuenta y cinco** (*55*) **sesenta y seis** (*66*) **setenta y siete** (*77*) **ochenta y ocho** (*88*) **noventa y nueve** (*99*).

● Look at this example of two verbs* together: **quiero visitar** (*I'd like to visit*). It is formed by **quiero** (*I'd like*) followed by a verb in the infinitive* **visitar** (*to visit*). Other examples are: **quiero ir** (*I'd like to go*), **quiero viajar** (*I'd like to travel*). Other verbs you can use in this way are **necesitar** (*to need*): **necesito comprar** (*I need to buy*) and **poder** (*to be able*): **puedo ir mañana** (*I can go tomorrow*).

ACTIVITY 20

Read dialogue 3.4 and indicate whether the following are true or false:

1. Querétaro is less than 100 kms to the north.   T/F
2. Manzanillo is to the west.   T/F
3. Puebla is the furthest distance mentioned.   T/F
4. The shortest distance is 80 kms.   T/F
5. Puebla is over 50 kms to the east.   T/F

ACTIVITY 21

Write these sentences in Spanish.

1. I need to travel to Guadalajara.
2. I'd like to visit the cathedral.
3. I'd like to go to Aguascalientes.
4. Acapulco is far away.

 ACTIVITIES 22 and **23** are on the recording.

Culture

In most major cities in Mexico, banks open from 8.30am or 9am until 5pm and on Saturday from 9am to 1pm. Between May and September they often close on Saturdays.

To make a cash transaction in a bank, go to **la caja** (*the bank teller's desk*). If you want to change money, look for the sign **cambio** (*exchange*) with a list of exchange rates. You can change **dinero en efectivo** (*cash*) and **cheques de viajero** (*traveler's checks*). The teller might ask how you want the money, for example **en billetes de veinte** (*in 20 peso bills*). You can take money from **el cajero automático** (*ATM, cash dispenser*) using your credit card with a PIN.

Post offices have similar opening times to banks. If you want to send a package, say **Quiero mandar este paquete** (*I'd like to mail this package*) and where you wish to mail it (**a los Estados Unidos** – *to the U.S.*; **al Reino Unido** – *to the United Kingdom, etc.*). If you want to send a fax, say **¿Puedo mandar un fax?** (*Can I send a fax?*).

If you take a cab, check that the cab's meter is set before you start. Get a rough price before starting the journey, especially if there is no meter or it is not functioning, by asking **¿Cuánto es a _____?** (*How much is it to _____?*).

For bus journeys pay the driver on the bus. Try to have the right money ready as you board – they usually charge a flat fare. Buses are not normally obliged to stop at every bus stop so make sure you indicate clearly to the driver if you need a bus. Check whether the city you are in offers **un abono de ahorro de transporte**, as in Mexico City, which is a 15-day card system for buses and metro. Aside of the regular buses, Mexico has a system of minibuses called **peseros**, **colectivos**, **combis** or **micros**.

If you need a police station, ask for **la delegación de policía más cercana** (*the nearest police station*). In smaller towns or villages you will need **la Policía Municipal** (*the municipal police*) or **la Policía**

Estatal (*the State Police*). To report something, say **Quiero hacer una denuncia** (*I want to report something*).

A list of **farmacias** (*pharmacies*) which offer emergency service is displayed in local pharmacy windows and local newspapers. Look for the sign: **las 24 horas**. If you go to one at night, ring the bell to get service. If necessary, go directly to **Urgencias** at the nearest hospital (**el hospital** or **la clínica**).

ACTIVITY 24

Test your vocabulary knowledge by matching up the columns.

la caja	bill (*currency*)
el cajero automático	fax
el dinero en efectivo	for hire (*taxi*)
los cheques de viajero	cash
el billete	pharmacy on call
el paquete	emergency room
el fax	bank teller's desk
libre	traveler's checks
la denuncia	package
farmacia de las 24 horas	report/statement
urgencias	ATM

Review 3

1. Match the Spanish phrase with the English equivalent.

1. **por aquí**   **a.** opposite
2. **todo derecho**   **b.** it's five minutes away
3. **la primera calle**   **c.** to the end
4. **a la derecha**   **d.** next to
5. **hasta el final**   **e.** in the area
6. **está a cinco minutos**   **f.** straight ahead
7. **al final de la calle**   **g.** the first street
8. **al lado de**   **h.** it's near
9. **enfrente de**   **i.** on the right
10. **está cerca**   **j.** at the end of the street

2. Write directions in Spanish to each of the places marked on the town plan.

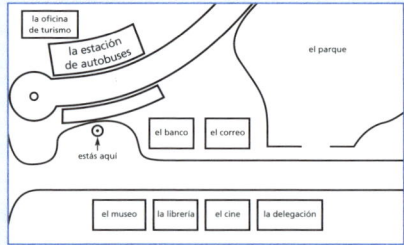

3. Fill in the gaps to indicate the location.

1. El banco está _____ correo.
2. La librería está _____ el cine y el museo.
3. El parque está _____ la delegación.
4. La oficina de turismo está _____ la estación de autobuses.

Time to Listen

4. **Listen to the recording and fill in the gaps.**

_____ . Quiero _____ a la estación de autobuses.

¿ _____ está?

Está _____ . Todo derecho y la _____ a la izquierda

_____ el final de la calle. Está a cinco _____ .

5. **Listen and choose from each of the pairs of options.**

1. The pharmacy is:
   a. next to the park/opposite the park
   b. five minutes away/ten minutes away
   c. at the end of the street/the first on the left

2. The police station is:
   a. between the movie theater and the bookstore/opposite the movie theater and the bookstore
   b. twenty minutes away/fifteen minutes away
   c. second on the left/second on the right

3. The post office is:
   a. in front of the park/opposite the park
   b. nearby/a long way away
   c. second on the right/third on the right

4. The cathedral is:
   a. 20 kilometers to the west/20 kilometers to the east
   b. next to a park/in front of a park
   c. nearby/a long way away

Time to talk

6. You're asking someone for directions. Follow the prompts in English and complete the dialogue.

(Say excuse me and ask if there is a post office nearby.)
Sí, hay uno cerca.
(Ask where it is.)
Está a cinco minutos. Todo derecho, la primera a la derecha.
(Say thank you and ask if there is a bank nearby.)
Sí. Hay un banco enfrente de la farmacia.
(Say thank you very much and ask if there is a museum nearby.)
Sí hay un museo.
(Ask if it is far.)
No, está a diez minutos; la segunda a la derecha.
(Say thank you.)

7. Test your progress in Unit 3. How would you say …?

a. 'Excuse me' and ask if there is a bank in the area.
b. 'straight ahead, the first street on the left and to the end'
c. that something is nearby
d. that the cathedral is five minutes away
e. that the bank is next to the post office
f. that the pharmacy is opposite the movie theater
g. that the museum is in front of the park
h. that the bus station is on the edge of town
i. that you want to visit Mexico City.
j. that Puebla is to the east; it's 80 kilometers away.

You can check your answers on the recording.

Going places

In this unit you will learn how to:

- ask and tell the time
- buy tickets for transportation and movies
- find out about departure and arrival times
- find out about starting/finishing times and
  opening/closing times

Listen to the recordings several times before reading
the transcripts. You may think you haven't understood
much, but keep going. Get used to the rhythms and
structures of the spoken language and use the
transcripts as consolidation afterwards.

ACTIVITY 1 is on the recording.

DIALOGUE 4.1

■ Buenos días. Quiero un boleto para Guadalajara.
■ ¿Para hoy?
■ No, para mañana por la tarde.
■ ¿De ida y vuelta?
■ Sí. ¿A qué hora sale?
■ A las tres de la tarde.
■ ¿Y a qué hora llega?
■ Llega a las seis.

VOCABULARY

el boleto	ticket
¿para hoy?	for today?
mañana	tomorrow
(por) la tarde	(in the) afternoon
de ida y vuelta	round-trip (*ticket*)
¿a qué hora?	at what time?
sale (verb **salir**)	it leaves (to leave)
a las tres	at three o'clock
llega (verb **llegar**)	it arrives (to arrive)

(!)

• Time is expressed as follows: **la una** (*1 o'clock*), **las dos** (*2 o'clock*), **las tres** (*3 o'clock*), etc. **Las diez de la mañana** means *10 o'clock in the morning* and **las cuatro de la tarde** means *4 in the afternoon*; **las once de la noche** means *11 in the evening*. For *it's 9 o'clock* say **son las nueve** (literally *they are 9*). **Son** is from the verb* **ser** and is used for all times except **es la una** (*it's one o'clock*), because **la una** is singular*. When something happens *at* a specific time, use **a**, as in **sale a las tres** (*it leaves at three*). To ask *what time is it?* say **¿Qué hora es?**

• **para** means *for*. The examples from the dialogue are as follows: **un boleto para Guadalajara** (*a ticket for Guadalajara*); **¿para hoy?** (*for today?*).

ACTIVITY 2

In dialogue 4.1, the customer wants a ticket for Guadalajara. Choose the correct information about the ticket (a–d) from each of the following.

1. a. this morning
   b. this afternoon
   c. tomorrow morning
   d. tomorrow afternoon
2. a. at nine o'clock
   b. at three o'clock
   c. at six o'clock
   d. at eleven o'clock
3. a. to arrive at six
   b. to arrive at three
   c. to arrive at nine
   d. to arrive at eleven.

ACTIVITY 3

Now write or say these times in Spanish.

1. At six o'clock in the morning.
2. It's four o'clock in the afternoon.
3. It's nine o'clock in the evening.
4. At eleven o'clock at night.
5. At three o'clock in the afternoon.
6. It's one o'clock in the afternoon.

ACTIVITY 4

Match the questions with the answers.

1. ¿A qué hora sale el autobús para Puebla?
2. ¿Qué hora es?
3. ¿Hay un autobús para Guadalajara?
4. ¿Sale por la mañana o por la tarde?

a. Son las tres.
b. Sí, hay uno a las tres.
c. Por la tarde.
d. A las tres.

 ACTIVITIES 5 and **6** are on the recording.

ACTIVITY 7 is on the recording.

DIALOGUE 4.2

- ▪ Disculpe. ¿Cuál es el autobús para la Ciudad de México?
- ▪ Es éste, el número diez.
- ▪ ¿A qué hora sale?
- ▪ A las tres y cuarto, pero está atrasado.
- ▪ ¿Qué tan atrasado está?
- ▪ Media hora.
- ▪ Entonces, sale al cuarto para las cuatro. ¿Cuánto tiempo dura el viaje?
- ▪ Dura tres horas y media. Llega a las siete y cuarto.

VOCABULARY	
cuál	which
éste	this one
el número	number
las tres y cuarto	a quarter after three
está atrasado	it's delayed
¿qué tan atrasado está?	how long is the delay?
media hora	half an hour
entonces	so, in that case
el cuarto para las cuatro	a quarter to four
¿cuánto tiempo dura el viaje?	how long does the journey take?
las siete y cuarto	a quarter after seven

● Telling the time:

Quarter and half hours are as follows: **las tres y media** (*3.30*); **las tres y cuarto** (*3.15*), and **el cuarto para las cuatro** (*3.45*). For minutes, *3.10* is **las tres y diez**, whilst *3.50* is **diez para las cuatro**.

• In Spanish, there is no equivalent to am and pm. If you want to specify, use **de la mañana** (*in the morning*), **de la tarde** (*in the afternoon*) or **de la noche** (*in the evening*).

ACTIVITY 8

In dialogue 4.2, what does each number or time refer to? Choose from the list on the right.

a.	7.15	1.	The official departure time
b.	3.15	2.	The amount of the delay
c.	3.45	3.	The arrival time
d.	3½	4.	The actual departure time
e.	½	5.	The duration of the journey

ACTIVITY 9

Join the sentences together and add question marks where necessary.

1.	A qué hora	a.	dos horas
2.	Llega	b.	Puebla
3.	El autobús para	c.	dura
4.	Dura	d.	sale
5.	Cuánto tiempo	e.	a las cinco de la tarde

ACTIVITY 10

Write these times out in full.

a.	5.45pm	b.	6.15am	c.	10.40am
d.	3.35pm	e.	12.25pm	f.	1.55pm

 ACTIVITIES 11 and **12** are on the recording.

ACTIVITY 13 is on the recording.

DIALOGUE 4.3

- ¿Tiene boletos para la función de las siete y media?
- Sí. ¿Cuántos boletos quiere?
- Quiero dos. ¿Cuánto es?
- Son cien pesos.
- ¿A qué hora comienza la película?
- A las ocho menos cuarto.
- ¿Y a qué hora termina?
- Termina a las diez y cuarto. Dura dos horas y media.

VOCABULARY

¿tiene? (verb tener)	do you have? (to have)
el boleto	ticket
la función	performance (in a movie theater)
¿cuántos quiere?	how many (tickets) do you want?
comienza (verb comenzar)	it begins (to begin)
la película	movie
las ocho menos cuarto	a quarter to eight
termina (verb terminar)	it ends (to end)
dura (verb durar)	it lasts (to last)

!

- Note the conjugation of the verb* **comenzar** (to begin/to start):

comienzo	**comienzas**	**comienza**	**comenzamos**	**comienzan**
I start	you start	he/she/it starts	we start	you/they start
		you start (formal)		

- The verb **tener** works in a similar way, except in the 1st person singular:

tengo	**tienes**	**tiene**	**tenemos**	**tienen**
I have	you have	he/she/it has	we have	you/they have
		you have (formal)		

❗

- **¿Cuánto?** (*how much?/how many?*) changes its ending* as follows:

	Masculine	Feminine
Singular	**¿Cuánto vino quieres?**	**¿Cuánta ensalada quieres?**
	How much wine do you want?	*How much salad do you want?*
Plural	**¿Cuántos cines hay?**	**¿Cuántas mesas hay?**
	How many movie theaters are there?	*How many tables are there?*

ACTIVITY 14

Read dialogue 4.3 again and add the missing information.

1. The movie starts at _____.
2. The movie ends at _____.
3. The performance begins at _____.
4. The movie lasts _____.
5. The tickets cost _____.

ACTIVITY 15

Complete each sentence with the appropriate word from the list below:

comienza   tiene   dura   quiere   termina

1. ¿_____ boletos para la función de las nueve?
2. ¿A qué hora _____ la película?
3. ¿A qué hora _____?
4. ¿Cuánto _____ la película?
5. ¿Cuántos boletos _____?

 **ACTIVITIES 16** and **17** are on the recording.

ACTIVITY 18 is on the recording.

DIALOGUE 4.4

- Disculpe, ¿a qué hora abre el museo?
- Abre a las diez y cierra a las ocho de la noche.
- ¿Todos los días?
- Todos los días menos el lunes. Los lunes está cerrado todo el día.
- ¿Cuánto cuesta el boleto?
- Veinte pesos.
- ¿Hay descuento para familias?
- Sí, señora, el veinte por ciento.

VOCABULARY

abre (verb **abrir**)	it opens (to open)
el museo	museum
cierra (verb **cerrar**)	it closes (to close)
la noche	night
todos los días	every day
menos el lunes	except Monday
cerrado/a	closed
todo el día	all day
cuesta (verb **costar**)	it costs (to cost)
el descuento	discount
la familia	family
por ciento	per cent

● Days of the week:

lunes	**martes**	**miércoles**	**jueves**	**viernes**	**sábado**	**domingo**
Monday	*Tuesday*	*Wednesday*	*Thursday*	*Friday*	*Saturday*	*Sunday*

All days of the week are masculine (eg: **el lunes**). For *on Wednesday*, say **el miércoles**. For *on Wednesdays*, say **los miércoles**: **estudio los miércoles** (*I study on Wednesdays*). Days ending in **-es** are the same in the plural (eg: **los lunes**); others add **-s** (**los sábados**). **El fin de semana** = *the weekend*.

● Two new verbs: **abrir** and **cerrar**. **Abrir** (*to open*) is a regular **-ir** verb:

abro	**abres**	**abre**	**abrimos**	**abren**
I open	*you open*	*he/she/it opens*	*we open*	*you/they open*
		you open (formal)		

cerrar (*to close*) is similar to **tener** and **empezar**:

cierro	**cierras**	**cierra**	**cerramos**	**cierran**
I close	*you close*	*he/she/it closes*	*we close*	*you/they close*
		you close (formal)		

Está abierto means *it's open*; **está cerrado** means *it's closed*.

ACTIVITY 19

Read Dialogue 4.4. again and decide whether the following statements are true or false:

1. The museum opens for ten hours a day.   T/F
2. The museum is open every day of the week.   T/F
3. A ticket costs thirty pesos.   T/F
4. It costs less for a family.   T/F

ACTIVITY 20

Write down the names of the following:

1. The two days of the weekend.
2. The third weekday.
3. The first day of the working week.
4. The last day of the working week.

ACTIVITIES 21 and 22 are on the recording.

Culture

The most common way of getting around Mexico is by bus. You may hear people referring to buses as **camiones**. The word **camión** is commonly used for both bus and truck. The service is very comprehensive and if you buy a first class ticket you should have a fairly comfortable journey. All the main towns and cities are connected by a good service and fares are cheap. Pay out a bit more for the first class buses, which are more comfortable and less crowded than the 2nd and 3rd class buses, and normally have air conditioning and bathroom facilities. If you plan to take a long distance bus, buy your ticket well in advance to avoid disappointment. Check if you can reserve your seat in advance. It is useful to have a reserved ticket with a seat number (**una reservación**). If you can't do this, make sure you get there in plenty of time as you may have to wait until the bus arrives before you find out how many spare seats are available. This process is more difficult if you take a second class bus. If you find someone in your seat when you get on, say to the passenger: **disculpe**, **pero éste es mi asiento** (*pardon me, but this is my seat*), and ask the driver to help if necessary. Keep your ticket stub with you throughout your journey.

There are now very few passenger routes on Mexican railroads. Trains still travel on the spectacular route from Chihuahua to Los Mochis on the Pacific coast, and there is a tourist route from Guadalajara to the city of Tequila.

However, the Mexico City metro system is one of the largest and best organized in the world. It is also remarkably cheap to travel on. The trains have inflatable rubber tires that run on wide tracks, and so they are surprisingly quiet. Many of the stations are brightly decorated to reflect some aspect of the area they serve, and in the city center one of the stations has been built to showcase a circular Aztec temple.

ACTIVITY 23

Useful expressions and questions for bus travel. Match the following with the English equivalent:

1. **No tengo reservacíon. ¿Hay asientos libres?**
2. **Tengo reservacíon, pero no encuentro mi asiento.**
3. **Perdone, pero éste es mi asiento.**
4. **Quiero un boleto de ida y vuelta.**
5. **Quiero un boleto de primera especial.**

a. Excuse me, but this is my seat.
b. I'd like a round-trip ticket.
c. I don't have a reservation. Are there any free places?
d. I'd like a first class ticket.
e. I have a reservation, but I can't find my place.

Review 4

1. Match the Spanish word or phrase with the English equivalent.

1.	**cerrar**	**a.**	to be delayed
2.	**un boleto**	**b.**	to arrive
3.	**ida y vuelta**	**c.**	to close
4.	**salir**	**d.**	to end
5.	**llegar**	**e.**	to leave
6.	**atrasarse**	**f.**	ticket
7.	**costar**	**g.**	to last
8.	**durar**	**h.**	to cost
9.	**comenzar**	**i.**	round-trip ticket
10.	**terminar**	**j.**	to open
11.	**abrir**	**k.**	to begin

2. Times and days. Write these phrases in Spanish.

1. On Saturdays at three o'clock in the afternoon.
2. On Wednesday at 11.30am.
3. Friday at six in the morning.
4. Every Monday at a quarter to ten in the morning.
5. On Tuesday at 7.40pm.

3. Fill in the gaps with the correct verb from this list:
abre, cierra, comienza, termina, sale, llega

1. La película _____ a las cinco y _____ a las siete.
2. María _____ a las siete y _____ a Guadalajara a las diez.
3. La farmacia _____ a las nueve y _____ a la una y media.

Time to Listen

🎧 **4.** Listen to the statements on the recording and choose the correct response from those below.

1. Termina a las nueve.
2. Tres horas.
3. Abre a las diez.
4. A las cinco, pero está atrasado.
5. Quiero dos.

🎧 **5.** Listen to these times and number each time, in the order you hear them, from the list below.

a. 5.30pm   **b.** 3.45pm   **c.** 10.15am   **d.** 5.30am
e. 4.45pm   **f.** 11.15pm   **g.** 12 midnight   **h.** 1.35pm

🎧 **6.** Listen to these people talking about travel arrangements, movie tickets and gallery opening times. Circle the correct option for each one from the list below.

1. The bus leaves at 3.25pm/3.35pm/3.45pm and arrives at 5pm/5.05pm/5.15pm.
2. The museum opens at 10am/10.15am/10.30am and closes at 7.45pm/8pm/8.15pm.
3. The movie theater opens at 1pm/1.10pm/1.20pm and the movie starts at 1.55pm/2pm/2.05pm.
4. The movie lasts 90 minutes/105 minutes/2 hours 15 minutes and ends at 4.20pm/4.25pm/4.30pm.

Time to talk

7. Follow the prompts and complete the dialogues.

(At the movie theater ask what time the movie starts.)
Comienza a las cinco.
(Say you want two tickets and ask the price.)
Son cien pesos.

(At the bus station say you want a ticket for Puebla this afternoon.
Ask what time the bus leaves.)
Sale a las tres de la tarde. ¿De ida?
(Say no, you want a round-trip ticket and ask how much it costs.)
Son cuatrocientos pesos.
(Ask if they take credit cards.)
No, lo siento.

8. Test your progress in Unit 4. How would you …?

a. say you want a round-trip ticket to Acapulco
b. ask what time the bus leaves
c. ask where the bus leaves from
d. say 5.15 in the morning
e. say the bus is delayed
f. ask how long the journey takes
g. ask what time the movie starts
h. say the movie lasts two and a half hours
i. ask if the museum opens every day
j. ask what time the museum opens
k. ask if there is a discount

You can check your answers on the recording.

Accommodation

In this unit you will learn how to:

- check into a hotel
- make a hotel reservation by phone
- report a problem in your room
- talk about dates and periods of time
- check out and pay

Keep a vocabulary notebook. Pick a maximum of six or seven items of vocabulary from the same topic, learn them and write them in sentences. Go back to them again and again and practice.

ACTIVITY 1 is on the recording.

DIALOGUE 5.1

- Buenos días. Quiero un cuarto, por favor.
- Sí señor. ¿Para cuántas noches?
- Para tres noches. ¿Cuánto es por noche?
- Setecientos pesos por noche, con el desayuno incluido.
- Muy bien.
- ¿Su tarjeta de crédito, por favor? Gracias. Es el cuarto número ciento treinta y cinco. Está en el primer piso.
- ¿Hay elevador?
- Sí señor, aquí mismo, a la derecha.

VOCABULARY

el cuarto	(hotel) room
por (noche)	per (night)
el desayuno	breakfast
la tarjeta de crédito	credit card
el primer piso	second floor (US), first floor (GB)
el elevador	elevator, lift
aquí mismo	right here

- To say *for* a period of time, use **para** in both questions and statements: **¿Para cuántas noches?** *For how many nights?* and **Para tres noches** *For three nights*.
- To state a rate of pay or cost, as in *per night* or *a night*, use **por**: **setecientos pesos por noche** *700 pesos a night*.
- **Piso** means *floor* of a building.
- **Mismo** is used with various words to emphasize close proximity. For example **aquí mismo** means *right here*, **allí mismo** means *right there*, and **ahorita mismo** means *right now* or *immediately*.

ACTIVITY 2

Read dialogue 5.1 again and decide whether the following statements are true or false:

1. The client wants to stay three nights.   T/F
2. Breakfast is included in the price.   T/F
3. The price of the room is 600 pesos a night.   T/F
4. The client has to hand over his passport.   T/F
5. The room number is a hundred and twenty-five.   T/F
6. It's on the third floor (US).   T/F

ACTIVITY 3

Now complete these sentences using **por** or **para**.

1. Quiero un cuarto (por/para) seis noches.
2. Son quinientos pesos (por/para) noche.
3. Hay tres trenes (por/para) semana.
4. Estoy en el hotel (por/para) tres noches.
5. Quiere seiscientos pesos (por/para) día.
6. Quiere café (por/para) el desayuno.

ACTIVITY 4

A hotel desk clerk asks questions/gives information. Complete the gaps.

El precio es seiscientos pesos por _____ . ¿Usted quiere el cuarto

para tres _____ ? El cuarto está en el segundo _____ . Es el

cuarto _____ doscientos uno. El restaurante está aquí _____ .

El desayuno no está _____ en el precio. El bar _____ en el

primer piso al final del pasillo. ¿ _____ tarjeta de crédito por favor?

No _____ elevador, pero la escalera está _____ mismo.

 ACTIVITIES 5 and **6** are on the recording.

ACTIVITY 7 is on the recording.

DIALOGUE 5.2

- ■ Hotel Sol, buenos días. Soy Carlos. ¿En qué puedo servirle?
- ● Buenos días. Quiero reservar un cuarto.
- ■ ¿Para cuándo?
- ● Desde el día treinta y uno de marzo hasta el dos de abril.
- ■ Su nombre, por favor.
- ● Mi apellido es Tomlinson: T-O-M-L-I-N-S-O-N, y mi nombre es Alice, A-L-I-C-E.
- ■ ¿Y el número de su tarjeta de crédito?
- ● Sí, es Visa, número 4264 9381 4527 5386.
- ■ ¿Y cuál es la fecha de vencimiento de su tarjeta?
- ● Vence el cuatro del cinco.

VOCABULARY

¿en qué puedo servirle	what can I do for you?
reservar	to reserve
¿para cuándo?	when for?
desde	from
hasta	to/until
el nombre	name
el apellido	last name, surname
¿cuál?	which?
la fecha de vencimiento	expiration date
vence (verb vencer)	it expires (to expire)

● Dates – The full list of months is as follows:

enero	febrero	marzo	abril	mayo	junio
January	*February*	*March*	*April*	*May*	*June*
julio	**agosto**	**septiembre**	**octubre**	**noviembre**	**diciembre**
July	*August*	*September*	*October*	*November*	*December*

● Note that months are always written in lower case: **marzo** (March). You can say dates in two ways: **el día tres de mayo** or **el tres de mayo** (*3rd May*). The day or date is always preceded by **el** (*the*).

● To indicate start and finish dates, use **desde** (*from*) and **hasta** (*to/until*): **desde el dos hasta el cinco** (*from 2nd to 5th*).

ACTIVITY 8

Read Dialogue 5.2 again and write the following in English:

1. The start date.
2. The end date.
3. The credit card expiry date.

ACTIVITY 9

Form sentences and add question marks where necessary.

1. En qué   a. es Michael
2. Quiero   b. hasta el tres
3. Para   c. reservar un cuarto
4. Desde el uno   d. puedo servirle
5. Cuál es   e. es Johnson
6. Mi nombre   f. cuándo
7. Mi apellido   g. la fecha de vencimiento

ACTIVITY 10

Write these dates in Spanish:

a. 3/3   b. 24/9
c. 15/12   d. 17/6
e. 23/10   f. 1/2
g. 12/8   h. 5/11

 ACTIVITIES 11 and **12** are on the recording.

ACTIVITY 13 is on the recording.

DIALOGUE 5.3

▨ Recepción. Buenos días.

● Buenos días, tengo un problema. La regadera no funciona.

▨ ¿La regadera no funciona?

● No. Y la lámpara está rota también.

▨ ¿La lámpara de la mesita?

● Sí. Y también, la tina está sucia.

▨ Lo siento mucho.

● Y faltan toallas en el baño.

▨ Disculpe señora. Ahorita mismo subimos.

VOCABULARY

la regadera	shower
no funciona (verb funcionar)	it doesn't work (to work/function)
también	also, as well
la lámpara	lamp
está roto/a	it's broken
la mesita	bedside table
la tina	bath
está sucio/a	it's dirty
faltan toallas (verb faltar)	there are no towels (*literally* to be missing)
el baño	bathroom
lo siento mucho	I'm very sorry
subimos (verb subir)	we are coming up (to go/come up)

When you complain about something in your hotel room, it is usually about something not working, broken, missing, or dirty. Use the following:
If something doesn't work say **no funciona**: **la televisión no funciona** (*the television doesn't work*). If something is broken use **está roto**: **roto** is from the verb **romper** (*to break*). The ending of **roto** changes, depending on whether the

noun is masculine or feminine, singular or plural: *la cama está rota* (*the bed is broken*), *el espejo está roto* (*the mirror is broken*). Use the same rule with **sucio** (*dirty*): *las cortinas están sucias* (*the drapes are dirty*), *el cuarto está sucio* (*the room is dirty*).

Use the verb **faltar** if something is missing. If the item is singular say *falta una lámpara* (*there is no lamp/the lamp is missing*). If it is plural, say, *faltan toallas* (*there are no towels/the towels are missing*).

Here are more things you may have a problem with in your hotel room: **la cama** *bed*, **las sábanas** *sheets*, **la ventana** *window*, **la silla** *chair*, **el armario** *closet*, **la secadora** *hairdrier*, **la taza del excusado** *toilet bowl*, **el papel higiénico** *toilet paper*, **los ganchos** *clothes hangers*, **el ruido** *noise*.

ACTIVITY 14

Read Dialogue 5.3 again and decide whether the following statements are true or false:

1. The shower doesn't work.   T/F
2. The main lamp is broken.   T/F
3. The bath is broken.   T/F
4. There are no towels.   T/F

ACTIVITY 15

How would you complain to the hotel management about the following:

1. The window is broken.
2. There is no toilet paper.
3. The bathroom is dirty.
4. The light doesn't work.
5. The bed is broken.

 ACTIVITIES 16 and **17** are on the recording.

ACTIVITY 18 is on the recording.

DIALOGUE 5.4

● Buenos días. Quiero pagar la cuenta.

■ Sí, señora, el cuarto ciento treinta y cinco, ¿verdad?

● Sí. Eso es.

■ Son dos mil quinientos pesos por el cuarto, más el minibar, ciento cincuenta pesos. Dos mil seiscientos cincuenta pesos en total.

● ¿Puedo pagar con Visa?

■ Sí señora.

● ¿Y puedo dejar mi maleta aquí durante el día?

■ Por supuesto.

VOCABULARY

quiero pagar	I'd like to pay
¿verdad?	is that right? (*literally* true?)
eso es	that's right/that's it
el minibar	minibar
en total	in total
con	by (*literally* with)
dejar	to leave
la maleta	suitcase
durante	during
por supuesto	of course

● The expression **¿verdad?** is used in the same way as expressions like *is that right?* Here are some examples: **el cuarto 135, ¿verdad?** (*room 135, is that right?*); **usted es el señor Martín, ¿verdad?** (*you are Mr Martín, is that right?*)

● **¿Puedo …?** (*Can I/Could I/May I …?*) plus a verb* in the infinitive* is used to ask permission for something: **¿Puedo dejar la maleta?** (*Could I leave my suitcase?*), **¿Puedo pagar con Visa?** (*Can I pay by Visa?*), **¿Puedo cambiar el cuarto?** (*May I change my room?*).

ACTIVITY 19

Read Dialogue 5.4 again and state the following in English:

1. The room number.
2. The check for the room.
3. The check for the minibar.
4. The total bill.
5. The method of payment.
6. Whether the client is leaving town now.

ACTIVITY 20

Ask if you can do the following, using **puedo (poder)** plus the verbs shown:

1. Pay by credit card – **pagar/tarjeta de crédito**
2. Leave your suitcase – **dejar/maleta**
3. Dine in the hotel – **cenar/hotel**
4. Change room – **cambiar/cuarto**

ACTIVITY 21

The sentences in this dialogue are in the wrong order. Reorder them.

Sí señor, puede dejar la maleta aquí mismo.
No, cuatro noches en total.
Quiero pagar la cuenta del cuarto doscientos uno.
Aquí tiene. ¿Puedo dejar la maleta?
Bueno. Tres noches, ¿verdad?
¡Ah sí! Cuatro noches. Son mil novecientos pesos.

 ACTIVITIES 22 and **23** are on the recording.

Culture

The Mexican tourist industry contributes greatly to the country's economy. There are many different types of accommodations available, depending on the type of tourism or travel involved.

Hotels are either independently run or are part of international chains, such as Radisson, Holiday Inn or Marriott. The chain hotels tend to be very expensive, however, and if you are working to a budget there are a lot of affordable independent hotels available, both in the **Distrito Federal** (*Mexico City*), and elsewhere around the country. Look for the **H** symbol followed by the number of stars (1–5). If you really have money to burn, and require real luxury, there are also some **gran turismo** (*deluxe*) hotels in the larger cities. You will probably need to make an advance reservation if you intend to stay in one of the bigger, more expensive hotels. You can normally do this by phone, fax, email, or by way of the internet.

All hotels are required to display their tariffs at the front desk. In the smaller, privately owned hotels check out the room and whether the price includes breakfast or other meals before making a decision.

In some of the coastal resorts, such as Puerto Vallarta, it is possible to spend your vacation in a **condominio**, a **villa**, or a **bungalow**. Check out internet sites to contact these.

If you are on the road and require quality accommodations with a good restaurant, look for a **motel**.

Here are some of the things you may wish to ask for whilst staying in a hotel, although staff normally speak some English:

When you arrive at the hotel, go to **recepción** (*the front desk*) and say **Tengo una reservación a nombre de** ____ (*I have a reservation in the name of* ____).

To ask if someone has left you a message, say: **¿Hay algún mensaje para mí?** *Is there a message for me?*

If you wish to change your room, ask: **¿Puedo cambiar mi cuarto?** *Could I change my room?*

If you require a wake-up call, say at 6am, ask: **¿Puede despertarme a las seis?** *Could you wake me at six?*

If you want to know if there is room service, say: **¿Hay servicio al cuarto?** *Do you offer room service?*

For breakfast in your room, say: **¿Puede traer el desayuno a mi cuarto?** *Could you bring breakfast to my room?*

And finally, if you want the hotel to call you a taxi, ask: **¿Puede llamarme a un taxi?** *Could you call a taxi for me?*

ACTIVITY 24

Separate the following words and rewrite them to form four hotel requests. Add question marks.

llamarme las puedo despertarme servicio cambiar mi seis cuarto a al puede a un taxi hay cuarto puede

Review 5

1. Match the Spanish phrase with the English equivalent. Add ¿...? where appropriate.

1. verdad
2. aquí mismo
3. mi nombre
4. mi apellido
5. no funciona
6. por supuesto
7. faltan toallas
8. lo siento mucho
9. está sucio

a. it's dirty
b. of course
c. my last name
d. it doesn't work
e. isn't it?
f. there are no towels
g. just here
h. my first name
i. I'm very sorry

2. Complain about the following:

1. The bath is dirty.
2. The shower doesn't work.
3. There are no towels.
4. The mirror is broken.

3. Complete the following, using one of the following words for each space:

para, por, verdad, aquí, hasta, desde

1. ¿_____ cuántas noches quiere el cuarto?
2. Quiero el cuarto _____ el once _____ el trece de marzo.
3. ¿Cuánto es _____ noche?
4. El restaurante está _____ mismo.
5. El desayuno está incluido, ¿_____?

Time to Listen

4. Listen to the questions from the hotel desk clerk and choose the appropriate response from those below.

1. Para tres noches.
2. Desde el tres hasta el seis de abril.
3. Sí, aquí tiene.
4. Anderson: A-N-D-E-R-S-O-N.
5. Es Visa, 4378 9472 4658 5397.
6. Vence el cinco del cinco.

5. Listen to these dates and mark each one on the list below as you hear it.

a. 3/3   **b.** 12/9   **c.** 15/8   **d.** 6/1
e. 23/11   **f.** 5/5   **g.** 19/7   **h.** 20/2

6. Listen to this client booking into a hotel. Mark the correct option for each of the statements below.

1. The client wants to stay for 3/4/5 nights.
2. She wants to arrive on 6th/7th/8th and leave on the 9th/10th/11th.
3. The room is on the 1st/2nd/3rd floor (US).
4. It's number 113/213/313.
5. The total price is 1700 pesos/1800 pesos/1900 pesos.

Time to talk

7. Follow the prompts and complete the dialogues.

(At the front desk, say you want a room.)
Sí señor, ¿para cuántas noches?
(Say you want the room for two nights. Ask how much it is per night.)
Son setecientos cincuenta pesos por noche.

(Call the front desk and say your shower doesn't work.)
Ah lo siento; ahorita subimos.
(Say: also the bed is broken.)
¡Rota! Bueno, ahorita mismo subimos.

(Tell the front desk clerk you have come to pay the bill.)
Muy bien; el cuarto ciento tres, ¿verdad?
(Tell her that's correct, and ask her how much it is.)
Son tres mil trescientos pesos.

8. Test your progress in Unit 5. How would you …?

a. say you want a room
b. say you want the room for three nights
c. ask how much it costs per night
d. say you want to reserve a room from the 5th to the 8th
e. say the first three months of the year
f. say the 10th November and the 16th March
g. say your name is Anderson and spell it
h. say the shower doesn't work
i. say the lamp is broken
j. say the bath is dirty

You can check your answers on the recording.

Shopping

In this unit you will learn how to:

- shop for food
- ask for clothes in different colors and sizes
- say something is too big or too small
- find your way around a department store

Confidence is very important in learning a language.
Practice saying words and phrases alone when no-one
can hear you. Exaggerate pronunciation and enjoy
yourself.

ACTIVITY 1 is on the recording.

DIALOGUE 6.1

▪ Buenos días, ¿qué desea?

● ¿Podría darme un kilo de naranjas y medio kilo de plátanos?

▪ ¿Algo más?

● Sí, manzanas. Dos, por favor.

▪ ¿Dos kilos?

● No, dos manzanas, y un cuarto de uvas.

▪ También hay melones muy buenos. ¿Quiere?

● De acuerdo. Deme un melón pequeño.

VOCABULARY

¿Qué desea?	What would you like?
¿Podría darme ...?	Could you give me ...?
el kilo	kilogram
la naranja	orange
medio kilo	half a kilogram
el plátano	banana
la manzana	apple
un cuarto	a quarter kilogram
la uva	grape
el melón	melon
de acuerdo	OK, fine
deme (verb dar)	give me (*formal*) (*to give*)
pequeño/a	small

● To buy fruit or vegetables by weight, ask for them in kilos, half kilos or quarter kilos. For example: **dos kilos de naranjas** (*two kilos of oranges*); **medio kilo de plátanos** (*half a kilo of bananas*); **un cuarto kilo de uvas** (*a quarter of a kilo of grapes*). You can omit **kilo**: **medio de plátanos**, **un cuarto de uvas**. Note also the difference between **un cuarto** and **medio** (without **un**). For anything less than a quarter kilo, ask in grams: **cien gramos de jamón** (*100 g of ham*).

> ● To ask for something in a store, use the expression **¿podría darme …?** (*could you give me …?*). **Deme** (*Give me*) which is another form of the verb* **dar** (*to give*) + **me** (*me*) is also commonly used, but it's more casual.

ACTIVITY 2

Read dialogue 6.1 again and match the numbers or weights with the items.

1. Melon(s)
2. Apple(s)
3. Banana(s)
4. Orange(s)
5. Grapes

a. Quarter kilo
b. Half a kilo
c. One kilo
d. Two
e. One

ACTIVITY 3

Complete these sentences by selecting the correct number from the box.

100   ½   2   1   ¼

1. Quiero _____ kilos de manzanas.
2. Deme _____ kilo de plátanos.
3. Por favor, quiero un _____ kilo de uvas.
4. Deme _____ melón grande.
5. Deme _____ gramos de jamón.

ACTIVITY 4

Now ask for the following things. Use **¿Podría darme …?** when you ask.

1. Half a kilo of apples.
2. Two hundred grams of ham.
3. Two kilos of oranges.
4. A kilo of bananas.
5. Two melons.

ACTIVITIES 5 and **6** are on the recording.

ACTIVITY 7 is on the recording.

DIALOGUE 6.2

- Hola. Quiero una lata de aceitunas y una botella de aceite.
- De un litro no tengo. Sólo tengo de dos litros.
- De acuerdo, de dos litros. Y también quiero una caja de galletas.
- ¿Algo más?
- Sí, un paquete de chorizo. ¿Tiene latas de sardinas?
- No, no tengo.
- Entonces, una lata de atún.
- ¿Grande o pequeña?
- Grande

VOCABULARY

la lata	can, tin
la aceituna	olive
la botella	bottle
el aceite	oil
el litro	liter
sólo tengo ...	I only have ...
la caja	box
las galletas	crackers, cookies
el paquete	bag, pack, packet
el chorizo	spicy sausage
las sardinas	sardines
el atún	tuna
grande	big

- When referring to a one-liter bottle or a two-liter can , etc., use **de**, as in **una botella de un litro** (*a liter bottle*), **una lata de dos litros** (*a two-liter can*; literally *a can of two liters*). Note the word order and note also **de un litro no tengo** (literally: *of a liter I don't have*). You may hear the word **sólo** (*only*) with **tener** (*to have*), as in **sólo tengo botellas de dos litros** (*I only have two-liter bottles*).

• Note that **pequeño** (*small*) ends in **-o** or **-a** depending on the gender* of the noun* (masculine: **un paquete pequeño**, feminine: **una lata pequeña**), whereas the ending of **grande** (*big*) is the same in both masculine and feminine (**un paquete grande**, **una lata grande**). These adjectives* are placed after the noun.

ACTIVITY 8

Read Dialogue 6.2 again. What does the shopper want to buy?

1. A pack of _____ .
2. A box of _____ .
3. A bottle of _____ .
4. Cans of _____ , _____ and _____ .

Which of these items are not available?

ACTIVITY 9

Match the container or the quantity with the item. Some may have two or more possibilities.

1. **una lata de**   a. **vino**
2. **un litro de**   b. **aceitunas**
3. **una botella de**   c. **aceite**
4. **una caja de**   d. **galletas**

ACTIVITY 10

Say you only have the following. Example: **50 pesos – Sólo tengo cincuenta pesos**.

1. one cookie   2. sixty pesos
3. one bottle of water   4. one entrance ticket
5. a hundred pesos   6. two apples

 ACTIVITIES 11 and **12** are on the recording.

ACTIVITY 13 is on the recording.

DIALOGUE 6.3

- Disculpe, ¿tiene este suéter en blanco?
- No. Sólo tengo éste en azul, verde y rojo.
- Bueno, en rojo. ¿Puedo probármelo?
- Sí, por supuesto.
  […]
- Es pequeño. ¿Tiene uno más grande?
- En rojo no. En azul o verde sí.
- En verde. Sí. Ésta es mi talla.
- Muy bien. ¿Quiere algo más?
- Sí. Quiero un pantalón negro.

VOCABULARY

este	this
el suéter	sweater, jumper
en blanco	in white
éste/ésta	this one
azul	blue
verde	green
rojo	red
bueno	OK
probarse	to try on
más grande	bigger
la talla	size
el pantalón	pants, trousers
negro	black

- When you are in a store and you're talking about a piece of clothing, say **este suéter** (*this sweater*) if it is masculine, or **esta camisa** (*this shirt*) if it is feminine. If the items are plural say **estos zapatos** (*these shoes*) or **estas camisetas** (*these T-shirts*). If you're talking about an item but don't give its name, simply use **éste**,

ésta, **éstos**, **éstas** on its own (*this, these*). Note the accent on the initial **é**. Use **esto** to indicate *this one* in general; this is useful if you don't know if the item is masculine or feminine.

● Say **¿Puedo probármelo?** (*Can I try it on?*) if you need to try something on, such as **un vestido** (a dress). The **lo** means *it* and in this case is masculine. If the item is a feminine noun, like **una falda** (a skirt), say **¿Puedo probármela?**. For masculine plurals, such as **los zapatos** (shoes), say **¿Puedo probármelos?** and for feminine plurals, **las camisetas** (T-shirts), say **¿Puedo probármelas?**. If the sales clerk asks you if you want to try something on, he/she will say: **¿Quiere probárselo (la/los/las)** (*Do you want to try it/them on?*) If you want to keep it very simple, use **lo** for everything: **¿Puedo probármelo?** You will be understood.

ACTIVITY 14

Read Dialogue 6.3 again, and decide whether the following statements are true or false:

1. The sales clerk doesn't have the sweater in white.   T/F
2. The customer tries on a blue sweater.   T/F
3. The sweater is too small.   T/F
4. The blue sweater is the right size.   T/F
5. The customer doesn't want anything else.   T/F

ACTIVITY 15

Say the following in Spanish:

1. Do you have this skirt in white?
2. Can I try it (the skirt) on?
3. It's too big.
4. Do you have a smaller one (skirt)?
5. This one (skirt) is my size.
6. I want this one (sweater).

 ACTIVITIES 16 and **17** are on the recording.

ACTIVITY 18 is on the recording.

DIALOGUE 6.4

▪ Disculpe, ¿dónde puedo comprar una camisa?

● En la sección de ropa de caballero, en el quinto piso.

▪ Disculpe, quiero comprar zapatos. ¿En qué piso están?

● La zapatería está en el cuarto piso, señor.

● Disculpe, ¿ropa de señora?

◆ La sección de ropa de señora está en el tercer piso, pero también hay moda juvenil en el segundo.

● Gracias.

◆ Disculpe, ¿dónde está la sección de deportes?

● Está en la planta baja…. No, no, está en el sótano.

VOCABULARY

la sección	section, department
la ropa de caballero	men's clothing
el quinto piso	the sixth floor (US), the fifth floor (GB)
¿en qué piso …?	on which floor …?
la zapatería	shoe department
el cuarto piso	the fifth floor (US), the fourth floor (GB)
la ropa de señora	ladies' wear
la moda juvenil	young fashion
la sección de deportes	sports section, sports department
la planta baja	the first floor (US), the ground floor (GB)
el sótano	basement

● Note the use of **de** in **la sección de ropa de caballero** (*the men's clothing section*). Note also the word order (literally *the section of clothes of men*). Here are other examples: **ropa de señora** (*ladies' clothing*), **la sección de deportes** (*the sports section*).

• Note the construction **¿Dónde puedo?** + verb. For example: **¿Dónde puedo comprar ...?** (*Where can I buy ...?*); **¿Dónde puedo encontrar ...?** (*Where can I find ...?*); **¿Dónde puedo cambiar ...?** (*Where can I change ...?*); **¿Dónde puedo dejar ...?** (*Where can I leave ...?*).

ACTIVITY 19

Read Dialogue 6.4 again. Write down the correct section in Spanish for the following:

1. a pair of boots _____
2. a woman's overcoat _____
3. a pair of men's pants _____
4. a pair of shoes _____
5. a young person's skirt _____
6. a man's jacket _____

ACTIVITY 20

Say the following in Spanish:

1. The fourth floor (US)
2. The fifth floor (US)
3. The second floor (US)
4. The first floor (US)
5. The third floor (US)
6. The basement (US)

ACTIVITY 21

Complete these sentences by filling the gaps:

1. Por favor, ¿_____ puedo comprar un pantalón?
2. Quiero _____ camisa. ¿En qué _____ están las camisas?
3. La sección de zapatería _____ en la planta baja.
4. ¿Dónde está la _____ de moda juvenil?
5. ¿Dónde puedo _____ la sección _____ ropa de caballero?

 ACTIVITIES 22 and **23** are on the recording.

Culture

In **grandes almacenes** (large department stores), such as Liverpool, there are comprehensive **directorios** (store guides) on each floor. Each one indicates the floor you are on. Remember that **planta baja** means *the first floor* in American English and so **el primer piso** means *the second floor*, **el segundo piso** means *the third floor*, etc.

El centro comercial (large hypermarket or retail area) on the edge of larger towns and cities offers car parking and a wide range of products.

All larger stores and chains of stores accept credit cards but there are still some smaller stores (including small food stores) which may not. Look for the credit card signs on the door or ask before you buy if you have any doubts.

Mexico is famous for its colorful and vibrant open market places. The rich traditions of the Aztec, Mayan and Spanish cultures have all contributed to making many Mexican markets a rich cultural experience as well as places to make some remarkable purchases. These markets are an important way of life for the many cultures represented in Mexican society.

Markets vary in type. In Mexico City there are many different markets, each with its own range of produce, whilst in other markets in different parts of the country, you will find everything you may want together in one place. From food products and fresh vegetables and fruit to local crafts and traditional clothing, from antiques and books to tapestries and jewelry, you'll find it all. Prices are often cheap but it is quite common for bargaining to take place.

Shoe sizes differ from the US. Generally speaking, the men's shoe sizes in Mexico are approximately a size and a half below the US equivalent. So, a size 9 in the US will be 7.5 in Mexico. For women's shoe sizes the difference is more like two sizes and a half. So a size 7 in the US is approximately a 4.5 in Mexico. Take these comparisons as rough guides only. They may differ slightly between manufacturers.

Review 6

1. Match the Spanish phrase with the English equivalent. Add
¿...? where appropriate.

1.	deme medio kilo	**a.**	a can of olives
2.	de acuerdo	**b.**	I'd like these pants
3.	cien gramos	**c.**	give me half a kilo
4.	una lata de aceitunas	**e.**	it's too small
5.	sólo tengo uno	**f.**	I'd like this
6.	quiero este pantalón	**g.**	a hundred grams
7.	quiero esto	**h.**	where can I buy shoes?
8.	es pequeño	**i.**	do you have a larger one?
9.	dónde puedo comprar zapatos	**j.**	OK
10.	tiene uno más grande	**k.**	I only have one

2. Do the following in Spanish:

1. ask for a kilo of oranges and half a kilo of grapes.
2. ask for a two-liter bottle of water and a can of tuna.
3. ask the sales clerk if he/she has this sweater in blue.
4. ask where the sports section is.

3. Complete the sentences, using one of the following words
for each space:

más, dónde, quiero, esta, medio, en, de

1. _____ un kilo de manzanas y _____ de plátanos.
2. ¿Tiene botellas de aceite _____ un litro?
3. ¿Tiene _____ camisa _____ azul?
4. ¿Tiene una talla _____ grande?
5. ¿_____ puedo comprar zapatos?

Time to Listen

4. Listen to the sales clerks and select the appropriate response from below.

1. Entonces, quiero dos pequeños.
2. Sí, quiero un pantalón.
3. Moda juvenil.
4. No, el azul es grande.
5. De un litro.
6. No, doscientos gramos.

5. Listen to the sales clerks and fill in the gaps.

1. Está en el _____ piso.
2. No. Sólo tengo esta _____ en rojo.
3. También hay melones muy _____ . ¿Quiere?
4. De un litro no _____ .
5. ¿Grande o _____ ?
6. La sección de deportes está en el _____ .

6. Listen and circle the correct option for each statement.

1. The customer wants **a quarter of a kilo/half a kilo/one kilo** of apples.
2. The sales clerk has oil in bottles of **one/two/four** liters.
3. The sweater is **too big/too small/the right size**.
4. The sales clerk only has the pants in **black/white/blue**.
5. The sports section is on the **first/second/third** floor (US).
6. The sales clerk sends the customer to the **men's clothing/women's clothing/young fashion** section.

Time to talk

 7. **Follow the prompts and complete the dialogues.**

(Ask for two melons.)
¿Grandes o pequeños?
(Say you want small ones.)

(In a clothing store ask if they have this sweater in red.)
No; sólo tengo éste en verde.
(Ask if you can try it on.)
Por supuesto.
(Say it's your size.)

(Ask the sales clerk where you can buy shoes.)
En la zapatería.
(Ask where the shoe department is.)
En el segundo piso.

 8. **Test your progress in Unit 6. How would you …?**

a. ask for a kilo of oranges and half a kilo of bananas
b. ask for a quarter of grapes and 100 grams of chorizo
c. say 'OK, agreed'
d. say you'd like a can of tuna and a liter bottle of oil
e. ask if they have this sweater in green
f. say you want this one
g. say it's big
h. say this is your size
i. ask where you can buy a pair of pants
j. ask where the shoe department is

You can check your answers on the recording.

Answer key

Unit 1
Activity 2
1. T; 2. T; 3. T; 4. F; 5. T

Activity 3
any time: 3
morning: –
afternoon: 1
night: 2

Activity 4
a3, b1, c4, d6, e5, f2

Activity 8
días, me, se llama, gusto, llamo, gusto, llamas, llamo, tal, luego.

Activity 9
Buenos días. Me llamo Francisco González. ¿Cómo se llama usted?
Me llamo Javier Martín.
Mucho gusto.
Mucho gusto. Adiós.
Hola, ¿qué tal? ¿Cómo te llamas?
Me llamo Rosa. ¿Cómo te llamas tú?
Me llamo Daniel.
Hasta luego.

Activity 13
1. Pedro Pérez, Pilar Martínez
2. Pedro Pérez
3. Andrés Sánchez
4. Andrés Sánchez

Activity 14
1. soy 2. eres 3. es 4. es 5. es

Activity 18
1. Italia Turquía Argentina Portugal Francia Irlanda Japón Brasil Estados Unidos Alemania Perú Grecia
2. portugués brasileño griego peruano alemán irlandés estadounidense turco
3. argentina francesa italiana estadounidense japonesa

Activity 19
1. ¿De dónde es (usted)? Soy de Estados Unidos.
2. ¿Eres (tú) argentino? Sí, soy de Argentina.
3. ¿Es (usted) de Estados Unidos? No. Soy inglesa.
4. ¿De dónde eres (tú)? Soy australiana.

Review 1
1 1g 2d 3a 4e 5b 6h 7c 8f
2 AM: Soy mexicana; soy de la Ciudad de México; vivo en la Ciudad de México; trabajo en la Ciudad de México.
JA: Soy australiano; soy de Sydney; vivo en Londres; trabajo en Londres
JS: soy estadounidense; soy de Boston; vivo en Chicago; trabajo en Chicago.
3 a. Me llamo Ana Duarte.
b. Buenos días, señora Duarte.
e. ¿De dónde es usted?
c. Soy de Guadalajara.
d. Yo también soy de Guadalajara, pero vivo en Monterrey.
4 días / Buenos días / ¿Cómo está? / es / Mucho / dónde / Soy / vivo / vivo
5 1F, 2I, 3I, 4I, 5F, 6F, 7F

6 Patrick   Irlanda
John   Australia
Isobel   Escocia
Clark   Estados Unidos
Jane   Inglaterra

Unit 2
Activity 2
1F, 2T, 3T, 4T, 5F

Activity 3
buenos días	good morning
nada más	nothing else
¿algo más?	anything else?
quiero	I'd like
para mí	for me
¿cuánto es?	how much is it?

Activity 7
1c; 2d; 3a; 4b

Activity 8
a. Son treinta y cinco pesos.
b. Son veinte pesos.
c. Son quince pesos.
d. Son cuarenta y cinco pesos.
e. Son cincuenta pesos.
f. Son doce pesos.

Activity 12
1c; 2b; 3f; 4e; 5a; 6d

Activity 13
¿Hay menú del día? Sí, hay.
¿Hay pollo? Sí, hay.
¿Hay ensalada? Sí, hay.
¿Hay pescado? No. No hay.
¿Hay sopa? No. No hay.
¿Hay cerveza? Sí, hay.

Activity 17
– Would you like dessert?
• What is there?
– There's ice cream and crème caramel.
• I don't want dessert. I'll have a black tea.
• And I'll have a large black coffee.
– Here you are. Two black coffees.
• No. The coffee isn't for me. I want a black tea.
– Pardon me. I'll bring it right away.
• And the check please. Do you accept credit cards?
– Yes, sir.

Activity 18
hay / Hay / quiero / quiero / Quiero

Activity 19
1. ¿Qué hay?
2. ¿Hay helado?
3. Hay pollo y pescado.
4. No hay botana.
5. Hay helado.

Activity 22
Primer plato: ensalada / sopa de frijoles / jugo de tomate
Segundo plato: pollo asado / enchilada / pescado
Postre: fruta del tiempo / helado / flan
Bebidas: cerveza / café / agua / refresco de naranja
jugo de tomate (drink or starter)

Review 2
1 1e, 2g(¿...?), 3h, 4f, 5b(¿...?), 6a, 7d, 8c
2 a6, b4, c1, d3, e8, f2, g7, h5
3 1d, 2h, 3e, 4f, 5a, 6g, 7b, 8c

4 M1 Buenos días ¿Qué van a
   comer?
   M2 Quiero el menú del día. ¿Qué
   hay?
   M1 Para empezar hay jugo de
   tomate o ensalada.
   M2 Quiero ensalada.
   M1 Muy bien. ¿Y luego?
   M2 Pollo, por favor.
   M1 ¿Para beber?
   M2 Una cerveza.

5 3, 13, 4, 14, 9, 19, 6, 16, 2, 12

6 black coffee: M
   salad: M
   black tea: M
   soup: M
   fish: W
   lemon water: W
   crème caramel: M
   beer: W
   fruit: M
   orange juice: W
   ice cream: W

Unit 3

Activity 2
1T, 2T, 3F, 4T

Activity 3
1b, 2a, 3d, 4c

Activity 4
hay / por / aquí / calle / la / todo /
hasta / calle / hasta / calle

Activity 5
1. La primera calle a la izquierda.
2. El primer banco a la derecha.
3. La tercera calle a la derecha.
4. Todo derecho. La segunda calle a la
   derecha, hasta el final.

Activity 9
Disculpe. ¿Dónde está el correo?
El correo está en la avenida Goya.
¿Está cerca?
No. Está lejos. A quince minutos de
aquí.
¿Quince minutos?
Sí. Todo derecho. La primera calle a la
derecha. Hasta el final de la calle.
Gracias.
De nada.

Activity 10
1. Disculpe. ¿Dónde está la delegación?
2. ¿Dónde está la estación de
   autobuses?
3. ¿Hay un correo por aquí?
4. ¿Está lejos?
5. Todo derecho hasta el final de la
   calle.

Activity 14
1b, 2a, 3b, 4c

Activity 15
1. La librería está al lado de la
   catedral.
2. El correo está enfrente del parque.
3. La estación de autobuses está en
   las afueras de la ciudad.
4. La oficina de turismo está entre la
   farmacia y el cine.
5. La delegación de policía está lejos.

Activity 16
1. ¿Está lejos?
2. ¿Dónde está la catedral?
3. ¿Hay un corrreo por aquí?
4. ¿La farmacia está enfrente del cine?

Activity 20
1F, 2T, 3F, 4T, 5T

Activity 21
1. Necesito viajar a Guadalajara.
2. Quiero visitar la catedral.
3. Quiero ir a Aguascalientes.
4. Acapulco está lejos.

Activity 24
la caja bank teller's desk
el cajero automático ATM
el dinero en efectivo cash
los cheques de viajero traveler's checks
el billete bill (currency)
el paquete package
el fax fax
libre for hire (taxi)
la denuncia report/statement
farmacia de las 24 horas pharmacy on call
urgencias emergency room

Review 3
1 1e, 2f, 3g, 4i, 5c, 6b, 7j, 8d, 9a, 10h
2 Here are some possible answers:
   1. El cine – A la izquierda, todo derecho. El cine está a la derecha, enfrente del correo.
   2. La delegación – A la izquierda, todo derecho. La delegación está a la derecha, enfrente del parque.
   3. La librería – A la izquierda, todo derecho. La librería está a la derecha, enfrente del banco.
   4. El museo – El museo está enfrente de la estación de autobuses, al lado de la librería.
   5. El banco – A la izquierda. El banco está a la izquierda, al lado del correo.
   6. Correo – A la izquierda todo derecho. El correo está a la izquierda, al lado del parque.
   7. El parque – A la izquierda, todo derecho al final de la calle. El parque está a la izquierda.

8. La oficina de turismo – A la derecha; la primera calle a la derecha. La oficina de turismo está a la derecha. Está detrás de la estación de autobuses.
3 1. al lado del
   2. entre
   3. enfrente de
   4. detrás de
4 Disculpe / ir / Dónde / cerca / primera / hasta / minutos
5 1. The pharmacy is:
   a. next to the park
   b. ten minutes away
   c. at the end of the street
  2. The police station is:
   a. opposite the movie theater and the bookstore
   b. twenty minutes away
   c. second on the right
  3. The post office is:
   a. in front of the park
   b. nearby
   c. third on the right
  4. The cathedral is:
   a. 20 kilometers to the west
   b. next to a park
   c. a long way away

Unit 4
Activity 2
1d, 2b, 3a

Activity 3
1. A las seis de la mañana.
2. Son las cuatro de la tarde.
3. Son las nueve de la tarde.
4. A las once de la noche.
5. A las tres de la tarde.
6. Es la una de la tarde.

Activity 4
1d, 2a, 3b, 4c

Activity 8
a3, b1, c4, d5, e2

Activity 9
1d (¿...?), 2e, 3b, 4a, 5c

Activity 10
a. Un cuarto para las seis (de la tarde)
b. Las seis y cuarto (de la mañana)
c. Veinte para las once (de la mañana)
d. Veinticinco para las cuatro (de la tarde)
e. Las doce y veinticinco (de la tarde)
f. Cinco para las dos (de la tarde)

Activity 14
1. 7:45
2. 10:15
3. 7:30
4. 2½ hours
5. 100 pesos.

Activity 15
1. Tiene
2. comienza
3. termina
4. dura
5. quiere

Activity 19
1T, 2F, 3F, 4T

Activity 20
1. sábado, domingo
2. miércoles
3. lunes
4. viernes

Activity 23
1c, 2e, 3a, 4b, 5d

Review 4
1 1c, 2f, 3i, 4e, 5b, 6a, 7h, 8g, 9k, 10d, 11j

2 1. Los sábados a las tres de la tarde.
2. El miércoles a las once y media de la mañana.
3. El viernes a las seis de la mañana.
4. Los lunes a cuarto para las diez de la mañana.
5. El martes a veinte para las ocho de la noche.
3 1. comienza, termina.
2. sale, llega.
3. abre, cierra.
4 5, 2, 3, 1, 4
5 f, a, h, c, b, d, g, e
6 1. 3.25, 5.15
2. 10.15, 8.00
3. 1.20, 2.05
4. 90 minutes, 4.30

Unit 5
Activity 2
1T, 2T, 3F, 4F, 5F, 6F

Activity 3
1. para
2. por
3. por
4. para
5. por
6. para

Activity 4
noche, noches, piso, número, mismo, incluido, está, su, hay, aquí

Activity 8
1. 31 March
2. 2 April
3. 04/05

Activity 9
1d (¿...?), 2c, 3f (¿...?), 4b, 5g, 6a, 7e

Activity 10
a. el tres de marzo
b. el veinticuatro de septiembre
c. el quince de diciembre
d. el diecisiete de junio
e. el veintitrés de octubre
f. el uno de febrero
g. el doce de agosto
h. el cinco de noviembre

Activity 14
1T, 2F, 3F, 4T

Activity 15
1. La ventana está rota.
2. Falta papel higiénico.
3. El baño está sucio.
4. No funciona la lámpara.
5. La cama está rota.

Activity 19
1. 135
2. 2500 pesos
3. 150 pesos
4. 2650 pesos
5. Visa
6. No

Activity 20
1. ¿Puedo pagar con tarjeta de crédito?
2. ¿Puedo dejar la maleta?
3. ¿Puedo cenar en el hotel?
4. ¿Puedo cambiar el cuarto?

Activity 21
Quiero pagar la cuenta del cuarto doscientos uno.
Bueno. Tres noches, ¿verdad?
No, cuatro noches en total.
¡Ah sí! Cuatro noches. Son mil novecientos pesos.
Aquí tiene. ¿Puedo dejar la maleta?
Sí señor, puede dejar la maleta aquí mismo.

Activity 24
¿Puede despertarme a las seis?
¿Puede llamarme a un taxi?
¿Hay servicio de cuarto?
¿Puedo cambiar mi cuarto?

Review 5
1 1e, 2g, 3h, 4c, 5d, 6b, 7f, 8i, 9a
2 1. La tina está sucia.
    2. La regadera no funciona.
    3. Faltan toallas.
    4. El espejo está roto.
3 1. para
    2. desde, hasta
    3. por
    4. aquí
    5. verdad
4 3, 6, 4, 2, 1, 5
5 f, a, h, g, e, b, d, c
6 1. 5 nights
    2. 7th, 9th
    3. 3rd
    4. 113
    5. 1800 pesos

Unit 6
Activity 2
1e, 2d, 3b, 4c, 5a

Activity 3
2, ½, ¼, 1, 100

Activity 4
1. ¿Podría darme medio kilo de manzanas?
2. ¿Podría darme doscientos gramos de jamón?
3. ¿Podría darme dos kilos de naranjas?
4. ¿Podría darme un kilo de plátanos?
5. ¿Podría darme dos melones?

Activity 8
1. chorizo
2. crackers
3. oil
4. olives, sardines, tuna.
Sardines are not available.

Activity 9
1b, 2c, 3a, 4d

Activity 10
1. Sólo tengo una galleta.
2. Sólo tengo sesenta pesos.
3. Sólo tengo una botella de agua.
4. Sólo tengo un boleto.
5. Sólo tengo cien pesos.
6. Sólo tengo dos manzanas.

Activity 14
1T, 2F, 3T, 4F, 5F

Activity 15
1. ¿Tiene esta falda en blanco?
2. ¿Puedo probármela?
3. Es grande.
4. ¿Tiene una más pequeña?
5. Ésta es mi talla.
6. Quiero éste.

Activity 19
1. La sección de zapatería.
2. La sección de ropa de señora.
3. La sección de ropa de caballero.
4. La sección de zapatería.
5. La sección de moda juvenil.
6. La sección de ropa de caballero.

Activity 20
1. el tercer piso
2. el cuarto piso

3. el primer piso
4. la planta baja
5. el segundo piso
6. el sótano

Activity 21
1. Dónde
2. una, sección / piso
3. está
4. sección
5. encontrar, de

Review 6
1 1c, 2j, 3g, 4a, 5k, 6b, 7f, 8e,
9h(¿…?), 10i(¿…?)
2 1. Quiero un kilo de naranjas y
medio kilo de uvas.
2. Quiero una botella de agua de
dos litros y una lata de atún.
3. ¿Tiene este suéter en azul?
4. ¿Dónde está la sección de
deportes?
3 1. Quiero, medio
2. de
3. esta, en
4. más
5. dónde
4 4, 1, 6, 3, 2, 5
5 1. tercer
2. falda
3. buenos
4. tengo
5. pequeño
6. sótano
6 1. quarter
2. four
3. the right size
4. blue
5. third
6. young fashion department

Vocabulary

a	at; to; on
a cinco minutos	five minutes from here
a la derecha	on the right
a la izquierda	on the left
a las tres	at three o'clock
¿a qué hora?	at what time?
abril	April
abrir	to open
el aceite	oil
la aceituna	olive
aceptar	to accept, to take
adiós	goodbye
las afueras	the edge of town
agosto	August
el agua de limón	water with lemon
el agua (f) mineral	mineral water
ahora	now
ahorita	right now
ahorita mismo	right now
al final	at; to; the end
al lado de	next to
¿algo más?	anything else?
allí	there
amarillo	yellow
americano/a	American
el apellido	last name
aquí	here
aquí mismo	right here
aquí tiene	here you are
el armario	closet
asado/a	roast(ed)
el asiento	seat (in train, bus, etc.)
atender	to attend to
atrasado/a	delayed, late
el atún	tuna
Australia	Australia
australiano/a	Australian
azul	blue
el banco	bank
el baño	bathroom

el bar	bar
beber	to drink
la bebida	drink
bien	well, fine, OK
blanco	white
el boleto	ticket
la botana	bar snack
la botella	bottle
Brasil	Brazil
brasileño/a	Brazilian
buenas noches	goodnight
buenas tardes	good afternoon/evening
bueno	good, OK
buenos días	good morning
el café	coffee
el café	bar; diner
el café americano	large black coffee
la cafetería	bar; diner
caliente	hot
cambio	change; currency exchange
la camiseta	undershirt
la carta	menu
la casa	house
la catedral	cathedral
cerca	near
cerrar	to close
la cerveza	beer
el cheque de viajero	traveler's check
el chocolate	chocolate
el chorizo	spicy sausage
cien	a hundred
cinco	five
cincuenta	fifty
el cine	movie theater
la ciudad	city
la coca	Coca-Cola®
comenzar	to begin
comer	to eat
la comida corrida	quick set menu
¿cómo está?	how are you? (*formal*)
¿cómo se llama (usted)?	what's your name? (*formal*)
¿cómo te llamas?	what's your name? (*informal*)

comprar	to buy
con	with, by
el condominio	condominium
el correo	post office
las cortinas	drapes, curtains
cruzar	to cross
¿cuál?	which?
¿cuántos/as quiere?	how many do you want?
¿cuánto cuesta?	how much does it cost?
¿cuánto es?	how much is it?
¿cuánto tiempo dura?	how long does it last?
cuarenta	forty
el cuarto	room
cuarto/a	quarter
cuarto kilo	quarter of a kilo
(son) cuarto para las cuarto	(it's) a quarter to four
cuatrocientos	four hundred
la cuenta	check, bill
cuesta (verb **costar**)	it costs (to cost)
dar	to give
de	from; of
de acuerdo	OK, fine
de aquí	from here
¿de dónde eres?	where are you from? (*informal*)
¿de dónde es (usted)?	where are you from? (*formal*)
de ida y vuelta	round-trip ticket
de nada	you're welcome, don't mention it
debajo de	under
dejar	to leave
delante de	in front of
la delegación (de policía)	police station
la derecha	right
la denuncia	complaint, report
los deportes	sports
desayunar	to have breakfast
el desayuno	breakfast
el descuento	discount
desde	from, since
despertarse	to wake up
detrás de	behind
diciembre	December
el dinero	money

el dinero en efectivo	cash
disculpe	excuse me; *also* I apologize
domingo	Sunday
¿dónde?	where?
¿dónde está ...?	where is ...?
doscientos	two hundred
durante	during
durar	to last
el edificio	building
él	he, it (*m*)
el elevador	elevator
ella	she, it (*f*)
empezar	to begin
en	in, on
en (blanco/azul)	in (white/blue)
¿en qué piso ...?	on which floor ...?
en total	altogether
la enchilada	corn tortilla with meat filling and tomato sauce, topped with cheese
encima de	on top of
enero	January
enfrente de	opposite
la ensalada	salad
entonces	so, in that case
entre	between
es la una	it's one o'clock
escocés/escocesa	Scottish
Escocia	Scotland
eso es	that's right/it
España	Spain
español/a	Spanish
está cerca	it's near
¿está lejos?	is it far?
está roto/a	it's broken
la estación de autobuses	bus station
(los) Estados Unidos	(the) United States
estadounidense	from the U.S.
el estanco	kiosk
estar	to be
estar atrasado	to be delayed, late
estar cerrado/a	to be closed
éste/ésta/éstos/éstas	this one/these ones

este (suéter)	this (sweater)
el este	east
¡estupendo!	fantastic!, wonderful!
la falda	skirt
faltan (toallas)	there are no (towels)
la familia	family
la farmacia	pharmacy, drugstore
la farmacia de guardia	emergency service pharmacy
el fax	fax
febrero	February
la fecha (de vencimiento)	expiry date
el fin de semana	weekend
el final (de la calle)	end (of the street)
el flan	crème caramel
los frijoles	beans
frío/a	cold
la fruta (del tiempo)	(fresh) fruit
la función	performance (*in a movie theater*)
funcionar	to work, to function
las galletas	crackers, cookies
el gancho	clothes hanger
gracias	thank you
el gramo	gram
grande	big
los grandes almacenes	department store
el grifo	faucet
el guacamole	guacamole
hacer	to make; to do
hacer una denuncia	to report something, make a complaint
hasta	to/until
hasta el final	to the end
hasta luego	see you later
hasta mañana	see you tomorrow
hay	there is/are
el helado	ice cream
hola	hi, hello
la hora	time; hour
el hospital	hospital
el hostal	hostel
la ida	one-way, outward journey
ida y vuelta	round trip
Inglaterra	England

inglés/inglesa	English
ir	to go
la izquierda	the left
jueves	Thursday
el jugo (de naranja)	(orange) juice
julio	July
junio	June
el kilo	kilogram
la lámpara	lamp
la lata	(tin) can
leche caliente/fría	hot/cold milk
lejos	far, a long way
libre	free, available, for hire (*taxi*)
la librería	bookstore
el limón	lemon
el litro	liter
llamarse	to be called
llegar	to arrive
lo siento mucho	I'm very sorry
el lomo	pork
luego	then, afterwards
lunes	Monday
la maleta	suitcase
mañana	tomorrow
mandar	to send
la manzana	apple
martes	Tuesday
marzo	March
más grande	bigger
mayo	May
media hora	half an hour
medio kilo	half a kilogram
el melón	melon
menos	except
el mensaje	message
el menú del día	menu of the day
el mesero/la mesera	waiter/waitress
la mesita	bedside table
mexicano/a	Mexican
México	Mexico
miércoles	Wednesday
mil	thousand

el minibar	minibar
moda juvenil	young fashion department
la moneda	coin; currency
muchas gracias	many thanks
mucho gusto	pleased to meet you
el museo	museum
muy	very
muy bien	OK (*literally* very well)
nada más	nothing else
la naranja	orange
necesitar	to need
negro/a	black
no es para mí	it isn't for me
no funciona	it doesn't work
la noche	night
el nombre	name
el norte	north
norteamericano/a	(North) American
nos vemos luego	see you later
	(*literally* we'll see each other afterwards)
noviembre	November
octubre	October
el oeste	west
la oficina de cambio	currency exchange
la oficina de turismo	tourist office
pagar	to pay
el pantalón	pants, trousers
la papa	potato
las papas fritas	French fries; potato chips
el papel higiénico	toilet paper
el paquete	package
para	for
para beber	to drink
¿para cuándo?	when for?
para empezar	to begin (*for the first course*)
¿para hoy?	for today?
para mí	for me
el parque	park
el pasaporte	passport
pequeño/a	small
perdone	I'm sorry
pero	but

el pescado	fish
el piso	floor (*of a building*)
planta baja	1st floor (*US*), ground floor (*GB*)
el plátano	banana
la plaza	square
poder	to be able (can)
el pollo	chicken
por	for; through; by; per; around
por aquí	around here
por ciento	per cent
por favor	please
por noche	per night
por supuesto	of course
el postre	dessert
el primer piso	2nd floor (*US*), 1st floor (*GB*)
el primer plato	starters
la primera calle	the first street
probarse	to try on
la propina	tip (*in a bar or diner*)
¿puedo?	can I …?
¿puedo probármelo?	can I try it on?
¿qué desea?	what would you like?
¿qué hay?	what is there?
¿qué hora es?	what time is it?
¿qué quieren ustedes?	what would you like?
¿qué tal?	hi there, how's it going?
querer	to want (would like)
la quesadilla	snack of filled tortilla
¿quién?	who?
¿quieren …?	would you like …?
quiero pagar	I'd like to pay
el refresco	soda
la regadera	shower
el regreso	return
la reservación	reservation
reservar	to reserve
rojo/a	red
romper	to break
ropa de caballero	men's clothing department
ropa de señora	ladies' wear department
roto/a	broken
el ruido	noise

sábado	Saturday
la sábana	sheet (*for bed*)
salir	to leave, depart; go out
las sardinas	sardines
la secadora	(hair) drier
la sección	department (*literally* section)
la sección de deportes	sports department
la segunda calle	the second street
el segundo plato	main course
el semáforo	traffic lights
señor	Mr
señora	Mrs, Ms
septiembre	September
ser	to be
sí	yes
la silla	chair
sobre	above; on
sólo tengo ...	I only have ...
son las dos	it's two o'clock
son treinta pesos	that's 30 pesos
la sopa	soup
el sótano	basement, lower ground floor
soy (de la Ciudad de México)	I am (from Mexico City)
subir	to go up
sucio/a	dirty
el suéter	sweater
el sur	south
la talla	size
también	also
la tarde	afternoon
por la tarde	in the afternoon
la tarjeta de crédito	credit card
el té negro	black tea
la televisión	television
tener	to have
tercero/a	third
terminar	to finish
la tienda	store
¿tiene?	do you have?
la tina	bathtub
todo derecho	straight ahead
todo el día	all day

todos los días	every day
tomar	to take; to have; eat/drink
el tomate	tomato
la tortilla	tortilla
trabajar	to work
el trabajo	job, work
las tres y cuarto	a quarter after three
tú	you (*singular*) (*informal*)
el turismo	tourism
las urgencias	hospital emergency room
usted	you (*formal*)
ustedes	you (*plural*) (*formal*)
la uva	grape
vencer	to expire (*credit card*)
la ventana	window
¿verdad?	right? (*literally* true?)
verde	green
viajar	to travel
el viaje	journey
viernes	Friday
el vino blanco	white wine
el vino de la casa	house wine
el vino tinto	red wine
visitar	to visit
vivir	to live
y	and
¿y tú?	and you?
yo	I
(la sección de) zapatería	shoe department
los zapatos	shoes
el zócalo	main square

Grammar summary

Articles

The form of the article is determined by the number and gender of the noun that follows.

Definite article

	SINGULAR	PLURAL
MASCULINE	**el** libro	**los** libros
FEMININE	**la** casa	**las** casas

The masculine definite article is contracted when it is preceded by the preposition a or de.

a + el = **al**   Voy **al** cine
de + el = **del**   El coche **del** camarero

Indefinite article

	SINGULAR	PLURAL
MASCULINE	**un** cine	**unos** cines
FEMININE	**una** casa	**unas** casas

The plural form of the indefinite article is translated as 'some'.

Nouns

In Spanish, all nouns are identified as either masculine or feminine. Gender can be identified by the form of the definite article – el, los (masculine) and la, las (feminine) – or the indefinite article – un, unos (masculine) and una, unas (feminine).
Nouns ending in -o are usually masculine and those endings in -a are usually feminine, but there are many exceptions to this and in order to remember which gender they belong to, it's best to learn nouns alongside the article.

Plural

For nouns ending in a vowel, add **-s**:

el helado   los helado**s**
la casa   las casa**s**
el boleto   los boleto**s**

For nouns ending in a consonant add **-es**.

el hospital   los hospital**es**

Personal pronouns

Subject pronouns

	singular		*plural*	
	masculine	*feminine*	*masculine*	*feminine*
I/we	yo	yo	nosotros	nosotras
you (*informal*)	tú	tú	ustedes	ustedes
you (*formal*)	usted	usted	ustedes	ustedes
he/she/it/they	él	ella	ellos	ellas

Yo soy mexicano. I'm Mexican.
Ellas son de Guadalajara. They're from Guadalajara.
Note that the 3rd person singular usted is used for formal address, but the 3rd person plural ustedes is used for both formal and informal address.
Note: Ud/Vd, Uds/Vds are the written abbreviations of usted/ustedes
Subject pronouns are generally omitted in conversation.

Direct object pronouns

	singular		*plural*	
	masculine	*feminine*	*masculine*	*feminine*
me/us	me	me	nos	nos
you (*informal*)	te	te	los	las
you (*formal*)	lo	la	los	las
him/her/it/them	lo	la	los	las

La compro en la tienda. I buy it in the store.

Indirect object pronouns

	singular		*plural*	
	masculine	*feminine*	*masculine*	*feminine*
(to/for) me/us	me	me	nos	nos
(to/for) you (*informal*)	te	te	les	les
(to/for) you (*formal*)	lo	la	los	las
(to/for) him/her/it/them	le/se	le/se	les/se	les/se

Mi madre **nos** da café. My mother gives *us* coffee.

Possessive adjectives and pronouns

Possessive adjectives (*my, your*, etc.) and pronouns (*mine, yours*, etc.) agree in number and gender with the noun to which they refer and not with the 'possessor'.

Mi casa está en Puebla. My house is in Puebla.
Mis padres están en Monterrey. My parents are in Monterrey.

Possessive adjectives	*singular*	*plural*
my	mi	mis
your (*singular*)	tu	tus
his/her/its/your (*formal singular*)	su	sus
our	nuestro/a	nuestros/as
their/your (*plural*)	su	sus

Possessive pronouns	*singular*	*plural*
mine	mío/a	míos/as
yours (*singular*)	tuyo/a	tuyos/as
his/her/its/yours (*formal singular*)	suyo/a	suyos/as
ours	nuestro/a	nuestros/as
theirs/yours (*plural*)	suyo/a	suyos/as

Mi casa está en Puebla. My house is in Puebla.
La mía está en Monterrey. Mine is in Monterrey.

Prepositions

por	through, around	sin	without	contra	against
al lado de	next to	hasta	until, to	de	from, since
a	to, at	cerca de	near	lejos de	far from
enfrente de	opposite	detrás de	behind	debajo de	under
entre	between	en	in, on	encima de	on
delante de	in front of	a	on, at	después de	after
con	with	para	for	desde	from, since

Note that the preposition a + el forms **al** and the preposition de + el forms **del**:
Mi casa está **al** lado **del** río. My house is next to the river.

Adjectives

Adjectives normally follow the noun they describe and agree with it in gender and number.
Adjectives ending in -o change as follows:

el restaurante buen**o**   los restaurantes buen**os**
la casa buen**a**   las casas buen**as**

With the exception of adjectives of nationality, adjectives ending in -e or a consonant have the same form in both masculine and feminine singular. In the plural, -s is added to those ending in -e and -es is added to those ending in a consonant:

el chico/la chica inteligente   los chicos/las chicas inteligente**s**
el carro azul   los carros azul**es**
la bicicleta azul   las bicicletas azul**es**

Adjectives of nationality ending in a consonant change as follows:

el señor francés   los señores franceses
la señora francesa   las señoras francesas

Verbs

Regular verbs

The infinitive forms of regular verbs end in -ar, -er, or -ir and are conjugated in the present tense as follows:

trabajar (to work)		**comer** (to eat)		**vivir** (to live)	
trabajo	trabajamos	como	comimos	vivo	vivimos
trabajas		comes		vives	
trabaja	trabajan	come	comen	vive	viven

Radical changing verbs

These are verbs that are regular in their endings but which undergo a change in the stem in certain persons:

Verbs that undergo a vowel change:
e – ie = querer (to want) – quiero
cerrar (to close), empezar (to begin), comenzar (to begin), pensar (to think), preferir (to prefer)
o – ue = volver (to return) – vuelvo
costar (to cost), poder (to be able), dormir (to sleep), doler (to hurt)
u – ue = jugar (to play) – juego
e – i = vestir (to dress) – visto
seguir (to follow), repetir (to repeat)

Verbs that undergo a consonant change in the first person singular:
c – zc = parecer (to appear): parezco, pareces
ofrecer (to offer)
c – g = hacer (to make/to do): hago, haces
l – lg = salir (to leave/to go out): salgo, sales
n – ng = poner (to put): pongo, pones

Verbs that add **g** to the first person only, and change a vowel in the second and third person singular and third person plural:

tener (to have)		**venir** (to come)	
tengo	tenemos	vengo	venimos
tienes		vienes	
tiene	tienen	viene	vienen

Verbs that change in the first person singular:
e – ig:
traer (to bring)

tra**ig**o	traemos
traes	
trae	traen

Verbs which are completely irregular in all persons

ir (to go)		**ser** (to be)		**estar** (to be)	
voy	vamos	soy	somos	estoy	estamos
vas		eres		estás	
va	van	es	son	está	están

Reflexive verbs

These are verbs like levantarse (to get up), where se means 'oneself' [*literally* 'to get oneself up' or 'to raise oneself'].
Reflexive verbs take the endings of the relevant verb group (-ar, -er, or -ir).
levantarse (to get up)

(yo) **me** levant**o**	(nosotros/as) **nos** levant**amos**
(tú) **te** levant**as**	(vosotros/as) **os** levant**áis**
(él/ella/usted) **se** levant**a**	(ellos/ellas/ustedes) **se** levant**an**

acostarse (to go to bed), bañarse (to bathe), vestirse (to dress), lavarse (to have a wash)

Use of the present tense

The present tense can express an action that is happening at the moment, or a habitual action:

Voy al hotel.	I'm going to the hotel.
Voy a la playa los veranos.	I go to the beach in the summer.

The imperative

The most useful form of the imperative for travelers is the formal imperative.
This is used as a polite form of address in stores and when asking for directions in the street. It uses the formal usted form, as in these examples:
Firme aquí, por favor. (Could you) sign here please?
Siga esta calle. Follow this street.

ser and estar (to be)

Spanish has two verbs meaning 'to be': ser and estar.
ser is used:
– to describe a permanent state:
Soy profesor. I'm a teacher.
La casa **es** grande. The house is big.
– to tell the time:
Son las dos. It's two o'clock.

estar is used:
– to describe position or location, or a temporary state:
¿Dónde **está** tu pueblo? Where is your town?
Estoy enfermo. I'm ill.

Verbs followed by an infinitive
These verbs are followed by the infinitive:
poder (to be able), querer (to want), necesitar (to need):
¿Puede traer la cuenta? Can you bring the check?
Quiero cambiar el cuarto. I'd like to change room.
Necesito comprar un boleto. I need to buy a ticket.

Note these other constructions which also take the infinitive:
Tengo que ir al dentista. I have to go to the dentist.
Hay que reservar el asiento. It's necessary to reserve your seat.

Other verb constructions
hacer is used to describe the weather:
Hace sol. It's sunny.

gustar is used to express likes and dislikes. It is used with an indirect object pronoun:
Me gusta el teatro. I like the theater. (*literally* the theater pleases me)

Questions

In writing, questions are indicated by an inverted question mark at the beginning and a normal question mark at the end: ¿…?
Questions are formed in three ways:

1. By using a question word or phrase: ¿Cuándo …? (When …?), ¿Dónde …? (Where …?), ¿Quién …? (Who …?), ¿Qué …? (What …?), ¿Cómo …? (How …?), ¿A qué hora …? (What time …?):
¿Qué haces? What are you doing?
2. By inverting the subject and the verb in the sentence:
¿Estudia Juan en la universidad? Does Juan study at the university?
3. By using the same word order as a simple statement, but with a rising intonation at the end of the sentence:
¿María trabaja los sábados? Does María work on Saturdays?

Glossary of grammatical terms

Adjective

A word which describes a noun or pronoun, giving information about its shape, color, size, etc., e.g. rojo (red), azul (blue), grande (big), pequeño (small).
El suéter es grande. The sweater is big.

Adverb

A word used to give information about a verb – expressing the manner, frequency, time, place or extent of an action, e.g. rápidamente (quickly), siempre (always).

Trabaja rápidamente. He works quickly.
Siempre llega tarde. He always arrives late.

Agree

To match another word in number (*singular* or *plural*), gender (*masculine*, *feminine*), or grammatical person (*I*, *you*, *he*, *we*, etc.).

Article

See **Definite article** and **Indefinite article**

Definite article

The English the definite article is 'the'. In Spanish, the definite articles are el (masculine), la (feminine) – and in the plural los (masculine), las (feminine).

Diphthong

A combination of two vowels, e.g.: ei in veinte (twenty).

Direct object

The noun, pronoun, or phrase which is immediately affected by the action of the verb, e.g.:

¿Los zapatos? **Los** quiero. The shoes? I want *them*.

Ending

A letter or letters added to the stem of the verb to show the tense, subject, and number; also to nouns and adjectives, to show the number and gender:

Trabaj**a** en un**a** oficin**a**. He works in an office.
l**as** cas**as** grand**es** the big houses

Feminine

One of the two genders in Spanish.
See **Gender**

Gender

In Spanish, all nouns have a gender, either masculine or feminine. The gender of a noun can be deduced from the form of the definite or indefinite article used (el/la; un/una). Gender also affects the form of accompanying words such as adjectives, possessive pronouns, etc.

Imperative

The form of a verb used to express orders or instructions, or to suggest that someone does something, e.g.:

llame una ambulancia	call an ambulance (*formal*)
pase, por favor	come this way please (*formal*)

Indefinite article

In English, the indefinite articles are 'a' and 'an'. In Spanish they are un (*masculine*), una (*feminine*) – and in the plural unos (*masculine*), unas (*feminine*), the equivalent of English 'some'.

Indirect Object

The noun, pronoun, or phrase indirectly affected by the action of the verb, e.g.:
Le escribe cada semana. She writes *to him* every week.

Infinitive

The basic form of a verb which does not indicate a particular tense or number or person, e.g.:

trabajar (to work), comer (to eat), vivir (to live), ser (to be)
This is the form you find in a dictionary.

Intonation

The pattern of sounds made in a sentence as the speaker's voice rises and falls.

Irregular verb

A verb which does not follow one of the set patterns and has its own individual forms.

Masculine

One of the two genders in Spanish.
See **Gender**

Negative

A negative statement asserts that something is not the case, for example by using 'not' in English. In Spanish, negative statements are formed using no, e.g.:
No quiero café. I don't want any coffee.

Noun

A word that describes a person (*Peter, the man*), a physical object (*the table*), or a concept (*peace*).

Number

Indicating whether a noun or pronoun is singular or plural. Number is one of the factors determining the form of accompanying words such as adjectives, articles, and possessive forms.
singular: el hotel (the hotel), la casa (the house)
plural: los hoteles (the hotels), las casas (the houses)

Person

A category used to distinguish between 'I'/'we' (*first person*), 'you' (*second person*) and 'he'/'she'/'it'/'they' (*third person*) forms of the verb. The person is reflected in the verb:
(yo) trabajo I work (*first person singular*)
(él) trabaja he works (*third person singular*)
(nosotros) trabajamos – we work (*first person plural*)

Plural

Denoting more than one.
See **Number**

Possessive forms

Adjectives and pronouns used to show belonging, e.g. 'my', 'your', 'his':

Tiene **su** boleto. He has **his** ticket.
El libro es **mío**. The car is **mine**.

Preposition

A word (e.g. 'at', 'by', 'from') or phrase (e.g. 'to the left', 'next to') used before a noun or pronoun to show its relationship to the rest of the sentence.

El autobús llega **a** las nueve. The bus arrives at nine.
Los libros están **en** la mesa. The books are on the table.
El hospital está **al lado del** hotel. The hospital is next to the hotel.

Pronoun

A word that substitutes for a noun or noun phrase, e.g. *them* in 'I see them' (instead of 'I see the children').

Question word

A word or phrase used to form questions, e.g. dónde (where), cuándo (when).

Reflexive verb

A verb whose object refers to the same person as its subject, by using a pronoun to indicate the reflexive action:
Me levanto a las siete. I get up (*literally* 'I get myself up') at seven.

Regular verb

A verb that follows a common set pattern.

Singular

Denoting only one.
See **Number**

Stem

The part of a verb to which endings indicating tense, number, and person are added.
hablar: (yo) **hab**lo, (tú) **hab**las

Subject

The noun, pronoun, or phrase that performs the action of the verb, e.g. '*Alison* buys an ice-cream', '*I* am thirsty'.

Verb

A word or phrase used to express an action, process, or state of affairs.
Pablo **tiene** dos hermanos. Pablo has two brothers.
Trabajo en una fábrica. I work in a factory.